staircases

staircases
eva jiricna

Watson-Guptill Publications / New York

contents

introduction

introduction

Staircases are one of the oldest building elements in architectural history, though it would be difficult to date their origin precisely. They appear to change with architectural eras, reflecting the prevailing philosophies and symbolic languages, unveiling the talent and ingenuity of those who have created them. They respond to the type of society for which they were built and, among other things, inform us about the existing state of the arts, fashion and technology. They become landmarks and trademarks, a constant source of inspiration, a never-ending story; they have been and will remain a stimulus to new and different interpretations, as there can always be an innovative solution to a perennial architectural problem. Amongst all of the other architectural elements, staircases occupy a special position and can – and very often do – totally overshadow the building of which they are a part. The skill with which some stairs, past or present, have been built very often stretches the limits of human imagination. Sometimes it is the technical knowledge which sweeps us off our feet, another time the appearance, the form, materials, or specific detailing. Staircases are an integral part of our daily life, as much as a special event or a memorable experience. The associations connected with the stairs of the Paris Opéra or those sweeping sets in the Busby Berkeley movies of the 1930s fill an important place in our memories, where reality meets dreams.

At the most basic level, the main reason for the evolution of staircases would originally have been the necessity of overcoming the difficulties of changing levels as comfortably as possible. The geological formation of the earth presents us with hills and valleys, steep rock faces and shallow gullies, hillsides and plains which even a prehistoric man would have wanted – and needed – to explore, to conquer, to discover. Moving upwards very often meant moving to a place of greater safety, so consequently the choice could have made a

difference between life and death. It was therefore very important to move quickly – it is easy enough for monkeys to jump from one branch to another, supporting their bodies with the help of their strong prehensile tails, but not so easy for people. Since our balance depends on our feet, a horizontal ledge is a better bet, when it comes to stability, than a slippery slope, so it is not unfeasible to suppose that the first elements of what would eventually become a structural staircase could have been the result of the repeated impact of footprints following a route up an incline or down a slope, over time creating pre-historic 'treads' that made it easier to climb.

The recognition of such an unintentional process could quite easily have resulted in the impulse leading to the first consciously constructed element, something like a cross between a climbing aid and a rudimentary stair. As a matter of fact, all of these early examples – the random indentations in river banks, sand dunes, short cuts through hillsides, carved ledges or handholds in rocks – make up the early chapter in the story of stairs, prefiguring further development into staircases, ramps and, more recently, elevators, cable cars, funiculars and escalators: who can guess what is going to follow?

The rules of structure have come about naturally, and are manifested to us through the forces of gravity. Guided by simple rules of strict logic, structure never changes its mind, even if its interpretation can vary practically indefinitely. Similarly, man's imagination has no limits and his inventiveness knows no bounds. There is no need to go too far to prove this literal 'wisdom': the force of gravity pulls everything including our bodies towards the centre of the earth, however hard we might try to defeat this fact. Remaining in an upright position requires a certain skill and this constitutes a victory over the demanding will of nature. Man's improving knowledge of nature's laws makes it possible to retaliate with wit;

responding to and overcoming the law of gravity is certainly one of the successes of the human race. Talent, knowledge and even instinct have left us with stepped monuments of many kinds – the earliest carved out of earth or stone with overwhelming simplicity. It is hard not to be stunned by the mastery these remnants reveal. There are equally impressive examples from more modern times, whether created by the skillful hands of unknown masters or by well-known artists.

Since this is an introduction to a book on contemporary staircases, it is not intended to present a historical survey, nor should it be seen as an educational essay. It is simply a selective glimpse into the past, a look at the mixed bag of the present, and also an attempt to highlight those historical references that are still closely linked to the creative 'richesse' surrounding us today.

We can still see some examples of the earliest stairs in their original glory, and they usually lead up to a very high point, to reach the very top, to help us to attain the peak. Being 'higher up' can mean all sorts of things, for example a state of superiority or safety, of being in control, being in charge. Even animals instinctively head for higher places, specifically if that is where they can't be reached. What we have not seen, or experienced, stretches our imagination, initiates dreams of gaining the extra power or skill to achieve the unachievable. Naturally such qualities were attributed to the gods and supernatural powers residing in heaven, occasionally deigning to descend to the lesser mortals on the earth's surface, but keeping a sufficient distance by occupying only its highest places, for example Mount Olympus. The gods were the most powerful creatures imaginable: to cross them was inadvisable and no expense or effort to

The grand staircase at the Opéra in Paris, built in 1875 by Charles Garnier.

Top: The stepped terraces of the Inca city of Machu Picchu, Peru.

Above: The 'sea of steps' in the thirteenth-century cathedral at Wells in England.

A medieval street-cum-staircase in the Umbrian town of Todi in Italy.

please them was too great. To that end places of worship were built and designed to be reached by supplicants as much as by those who tended to the demands of the immortal ones. How else to get to elevated destinations but by climbing endless stairs?

There are numerous monuments which are solely a means of access to places of devotion, sacrifice and penitence. Fascinating staircases, among other things, have been built in order to reach such places. Those which are still in existence demonstrate that nothing was too expensive or too much of an effort if the task was to placate those who controlled mankind's very existence. Permanence was certainly an issue since people were always searching to secure everlasting life or to validate their claim to it. The impressive beauty of these structures remains with us even though the passage of

time has washed away most traces of the sweat, suffering, lost lives, tears and pain endured in their construction.

It is not difficult to understand that, when builders wanted to make stairs, the rules of their functional performance were instinctively or empirically applied, dictated on the one hand by the shape and proportion of the human body, on the other by the forces of gravity. The relationship between a tread and a riser necessarily dictates the angle of the stairs as much as the angle of a climbing body is dictated by the angle of a hillside or cliff face.

Ancient temples or pyramids in Egypt and elsewhere were often stepped. Sometimes the entire structure is stepped in two or more differing systems with different proportions. It has occurred to me that the aesthetics of the stairs themselves were so powerful that the

architects became obsessive about using their form wherever possible, not only because of the fundamental structural principle of a stepped plane actually holding the whole thing together.

In the first millennium BC the Etruscans in Italy cut stairs out of the earth to lead up to their temples and tombs. Two thousand years later, the massive stepped terraces of Machu Picchu (c.1450) in Peru formed a magnificent visual monument, and it could be reasoned that they also stabilize the hills they are built on. Another fact to remember is that in the ancient world symbolism was an essential element of architectural and artistic language, and the pyramidal shapes, their staircases and stairs generally were probably communicating much more than we can now decipher, even though the sense of astonishment and admiration at the skill and scale of the work involved remain.

An Etruscan staircase cut out of the earth, first millennium BC, northern Italy.

The early-eighteenth-century Cascade at Chatsworth House, Derbyshire, England.

To leave the introductory chapter on stairs without paying at least a token salute to one particular type of stair formation, landscape stairs, would leave the story incomplete. The Etruscan stairs illustrated here and the Inca city of Machu Picchu suggest a special skill of forming and re-forming public spaces by incorporating stairs in landscape. It is sometimes a very functional arrangement or a safety device but it can be equally rich as a result of a man's inventiveness and imagination. This concept was given a more urban treatment in the medieval Umbrian town of Todi, where a street doubles as a staircase. I do not know if there was an architect involved in the process, or just an ingenious local builder

following his artistic instinct and at the same time resolving the problem of excess water in the street. The result is so monumental, and practical, and so well executed, that one wonders whether to call it a piece of art or a simple, skillful solution. The combination of intelligence, care and the sensitive handling of a complex problem has resulted in remarkable, yet simple, perfection. This approach to stairs as landscape can also be found at the thirteenth-century Wells Cathedral in England.

Wells Cathedral invites its visitors to enter by climbing a veritable sea of steps leading to its entrance. Obviously a very difficult transition between the different slopes of the hill made the situation extremely awkward for

the builders to form just one main direction. Planes and slopes struggle with each other and eventually create a wonderful memorial to their own 'armistice'. Nothing is straight, nothing is perfectly horizontal or vertical. And yet the result is truly monumental and almost symbolic in its attempt to achieve the impossible. Probably not quite to the architect's satisfaction but, considering the date of its construction, it is nevertheless a remarkable solution.

Created about 400 years later, at the beginning of the eighteenth century, the Cascade at Chatsworth House, Derbyshire, England, is probably one of the prettiest and most unusual examples of landscaped stairs. A shallow hill has become the venue for a play-off

Michelangelo's
Laurentian Library
staircase (1524)
in Florence.

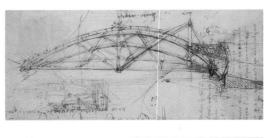

Top: A visionary design
for a mechanical
staircase by Leonardo
da Vinci.

Above: George Gilbert
Scott's Gothic Revival
staircase at the Midland
Hotel (1868–75), London.

between a static architectural feature made of an equally static material – stone – with the cheerful, changeable and dynamic element of water. Here are all the elements which belong to nature – grass, water, stone; man's contribution is imagination and skill. It is a monumental attempt but still modest enough to allow nature to maintain its superior role in the drama. Looking up, the view is terminated by the Cascade House, which can turn itself into a waterfall, and which can surprise the visitor with a sudden splash of water springing through the holes in the floor. But my favourite view is the one looking down the hill to where

the cascade disappears into the lap of the landscape: a great monument to the classical English garden.

About 200 years earlier, the Renaissance, with its emphasis on the wonders of man rather than nature, was a period in which remarkable skill was brought to projects that were heavy and substantial on the one hand, and light and subtle on the other. Artists began to be able to express their artistic visions in staircase form, with results as striking, and varied, as Michelangelo's Laurentian Library staircase (1524) in Florence, and Leonardo da Vinci's typically visionary design for a mechanical staircase. The elegant spiral also came into its

own during this period. One relatively simple example is the Great Cloister staircase (1550) at the Convento de Cristo in Tomar, one of Portugal's most important historic buildings.

By the Baroque period the staircase was so important that it was very often constructed in the same manner as a building, either attached to it or creating another building within it. Bernini's spiral staircase (1638) for the Barberini Palace in Rome is a good case in point. The careful juxtaposition of forms, details, even attention to future maintenance figured prominently on the architect's list of that era. Of course the time scale in which people designed buildings in those days was somewhat more luxurious than we are used to today.

Top: The central spiral staircase (1638) at the Barberini Palace, Rome, designed by Bernini.

Above: The nineteenth-century oak spiral at the Duchess Anna Amalia Library, Weimar, Germany.

The stone spiral staircase (1550) in the Great Cloister at the Convento de Cristo in Tomar, Portugal.

Established in the mid-eighteenth century, the Duchess Anna Amalia Library at Weimar, Germany, has always been as famous for its Rococo splendour as for its treasures. When, at the suggestion of Johann von Goethe, an addition was built (1803–5) linking the library building to the adjacent medieval City Tower, a remarkable spiral staircase was installed, the newel of which was formed by a single oak tree. The level of craftsmanship is beyond expectation for a 'simple' library.

The later part of the nineteenth century introduced an even richer palette of artistic and monumental staircases in private homes, opera houses, theatres, townhouses, museums and railway stations. The staircase of George Gilbert Scott's Midland Hotel (1868–75) at St Pancras Station, London, makes a dramatic statement in a romanticized Gothic Revival style. By playing with shapes and forms which were in the actual Gothic period a miracle of technology – when architecture expressed structural knowledge and structural performance in every single detail – Scott has achieved a powerful, if merely decorative, appearance. By the nineteenth century, the recreation of Gothic forms – once the proof of man's skill in stretching the technology of stonework to its limits – had become little more than the skillful application of tricks to create various, often badly understood, copies and pastiches of the originals. As a matter of fact, what could have better expressed the attitude of the 'infallible' Victorian society than this exaggerated, heavy-handed statement that now looks pretentious and uncomfortable to some, magnificent to others. In many ways Charles Garnier's Paris Opéra (see page 9), completed in the same year as the Midland Hotel, is probably the limit of how far such excess can go. The overexpansion of theatrical skill hardly allows the stair's engineering principle to shine through and the overpowering drama – with its sensuality, extremity, extravagance and exaggeration – could be compared with the extremes of the late Baroque period. Both fashion and architecture reached an apogee in this remarkable building, in a way a narcissistic reflection of the Second Empire society for which it was designed. Simplicity and simplification were terms that had almost vanished from the architectural vocabulary of that era. I say 'almost' because not all

Jules Saulnier's elegant steel spiral (1872–4) in the Nestlé factory, Noisiel, France.

Top: The Art Nouveau staircase designed by Victor Horta for his house (1898–1900) in Brussels.

Above: Henry van de Velde's staircase (1906) for the School of Architecture at Weimar.

staircases of this period had such grandiose aspirations. While the Opéra was being built in Paris, to the east of that city Jules Saulnier was designing a remarkable iron spiral (1872–4) for the Nestlé factory in Noisiel. The elegance and simplicity of the staircase, supported by a steel ribbon, is still impressive today.

Decorativism – though far removed from the Second Empire style – also formed part of the creative approach of the Art Nouveau master Victor Horta. His soft, loving and flowing touch seems to have made any material bend to his will, not least in the staircase for the house he designed for himself (1898–1900) in Brussels. Even if the nature of his work was somewhat affected by the influences of the past, his interpretation and his creations became unique, sometimes more symbolic than real. Fantasy again, but more human, more joyful,

free from the domineering Victorian approach. Only six years later, still a long time before the groundbreaking exhibition of Decorative Arts in Paris of 1925, the brave and simple staircase designed by Henry van de Velde for the School of Architecture at Weimar (1906) summarizes in one statement just how far technology had come for those who were brave enough to use it.

The amazing energy and inventiveness found in such examples as van de Velde's Weimar staircase can be seen as a transitional link from Art Nouveau to the most important movement in the twentieth century – Modernism. With the clarity of hindsight, it is easily understandable that the excesses, dogmatism and dictatorial attitude of the previous masters were bound to provoke rebellious artists and architects to come up with something new and revolutionary. The

intention to dispense with decoration, glamour and pretension was behind the new philosophy and the new architectural approach. Building on the tradition of Otto Wagner, Adolf Loos and generally speaking the entire movement of functionalism – perhaps the father or at least a close relative of minimalism – this approach was taken almost to an extreme. I myself was brought up in an apartment which was truly representative of Czech Functionalism, and most of my friends lived in a similar environment. Our parents' generation was committed to change, to the new way of life, not just paying lip service to a trend. Then, when I eventually became an architectural student, all of my professors were either protagonists or founders of that remarkable and short-lived era,

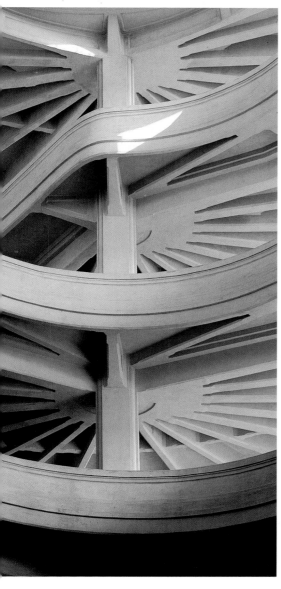

The concrete ramp designed in 1920 by Giacomo Mattè Trucco for the Fiat Lingotto factory in Turin.

The central staircase at Le Corbusier's Villa Savoye (1929–31), Poissy, France.

so nothing seemed more natural to me. We were steeped in the philosophy of the whole movement, and without a doubt this has shaped my whole view on design. I do remember how much I suffered when, due to unavoidable circumstances, I was obliged to live in the house of my mother-in-law, an art historian who collected antique furniture. It took me a long time to be able to appreciate the beauty of the old in other people's traditional interiors, especially when I came to England, where modern architecture and functionalism were much less common.

Staircases of the Modern Movement – perhaps because of the conscious decision to re-define structural laws, to reduce the excess – are examples of splendid aesthetics and very often a remarkable (if sometimes very simple) level of craftsmanship. With the First World War just behind and the hope of everlasting peace ahead, the potential of all the technologies invented for wartime purposes made it easier for the most daring thoughts and dreams to come down to earth. In 1920 reinforced concrete was brand new, and it was embraced by the brilliant engineer Giacomo Mattè Trucco for his work on the Fiat Lingotto factory in Turin – the first building to be constructed using this new development. The monumental concrete helicoidal ramp allowed cars to be driven from the factory floor to the rooftop test track above. The new techniques in concrete, steel and glass opened up new opportunities to design houses full of 'fresh air' – realistically and symbolically – letting in the light, leaving everything that was not a bare necessity behind. That was the intention, but another richness was created which has influenced architects up to the present day. It would be difficult to exclude Le Corbusier's Villa Savoye (1929–31), since it is a cornerstone of modern architecture. How could one overlook the sophisticated perfection of its scale and proportions, the balance of its straight and curved elements, culminating in

Top: The main staircase in Pierre Chareau's Maison de Verre (1930), Paris.

Above: Auguste Perret's impressive double stair designed in 1937 for the Social and Economic Council, Paris.

The De La Warr Pavilion (1933–6) in Bexhill-on-Sea, England, by Eric Mendelsohn and Serge Chermayeff.

its famous central staircase? This villa not only created a new vocabulary, but changed our approach to the perception of architecture for ever. Modern architecture is appealing to some, appalling to others. The influence of Le Corbusier's particular way of thinking, as well as that of his disciples, resulted in many remarkable examples of good architecture – and just as many badly interpreted monstrosities. Yet again, architecture had a chance to combine everything in its eagerness to express itself, with the interaction of artists, poets, writers and philosophers – but also engineers and scientists – as a matter of course.

One of the most extraordinary success stories of a little-known architect becoming a guru, a symbol, and an architect's god all in one person is that of Pierre Chareau, who achieved this status through the incredible Maison de Verre (1930), Paris. Was it the sophisticated client

(perhaps a frustrated architect who ended up a gynaecologist and therefore could afford to pay for his dream), was it the ingenious architect who had never had a chance to sparkle before, or was it a fortuitous collaboration between the two that produced such an outstanding result? Most of the architects of the high-tech persuasion (Norman Foster, Richard Rogers, John Young, etc.) dreamed about superseding this genius, though none of them has yet done so. The staircase of the Maison de Verre has obvious similarities with some of the other examples in this book, but look carefully. Chareau's work is not high-tech for the sake of high-tech – it embodies inventiveness and ingenuity combined with modesty, simplicity and subtle elegance.

The staircase in the De La Warr Pavilion (1933–6) in Bexhill-on-Sea, England, by Eric

Mendelsohn and Serge Chermayeff is a bravura performance by real virtuosi. How far could the skill of this partnership have gone, what other legacies could have been created, had the Second World War not cut off the blood supply from this union of mind and soul? The architects have achieved perfection from all viewpoints: the use of new technology and the design concept are so united that even the most conservative eye could not be displeased.

The wave of enthusiasm for new materials and technologies so prevalent in the 1930s is equally apparent in the work of Auguste Perret for the Social and Economic Council (originally the Musée des Travaux Publics), Paris. Built in 1937, the staircase is a remarkably well-made product. The last 60 years of struggle to advance the use of concrete have done little to surpass the elegance of structure or quality of

Top: A delicate modern metal spiral at the ancient El Zulfa Mosque in Oman.

Above: A sturdier spiral in a house in Bosques de Los Lomas (1990), Mexico, by Augustín Hernandez.

Carlo Scarpa's geometric steps at the Brion family cemetery (1970–72), San Vito, Italy.

manufacture achieved by Perret. The modesty of the design has resulted in a possibly unintended dignity. Every architectural student (not to mention the adults) should pay a visit.

It would be a glaring omission in any discussion of twentieth-century staircases not to mention the remarkable Carlo Scarpa, whose career spanned half the century. He is important not only for his contributions to modern architecture but also for his approach to the reconstruction and conversion of historic buildings. Scarpa developed a distinctive style of providing a readable history through his design, instead of occupying himself with a rigid theory of reconstruction. The staircase he designed for the Brion family cemetery (1970–72) at San Vito, Italy, shows brilliantly

his skill at reaching a monumental solution within a very limited range of materials, at the same time achieving a very simple appearance with very simple details. His ability to play with light and shadow help the overall effect to become exemplary. Scarpa's influence on architects of both new-build and historic conversions is still going strong. The addition of new staircases to older buildings is an increasingly common preoccupation with architects. In the house at Bosques de Los Lomas, Mexico, by Augustín Hernandez, an otherwise traditional-looking wine cellar is reached by a clever and sturdily minimalist metal spiral. By contrast, the lightness and delicacy of the modern metal spiral at the old El Zulfa mosque in Oman make it appear one step

short of imaginary. Modern technology and materials have made important-looking staircases – once restricted to the wealthiest and most powerful – available to a much wider range of people and building types. At a private residence designed by Charles Vandenhove in Namur, Belgium (see page 18), the elegant, controlled double staircase reflects the strict discipline associated with Belgium's recent cultural heritage, but still conveys a sense of timeless monumentality.

Perhaps one of the last realizations of pre-war philosophy, but in a post-war application, was the commission to build Brasilia, the city of the future – a dream brief for any architect. Was it pure coincidence that a Czech-born head of state, Juscelino Kubitschek, and a

The Itamaraty Palace (1958), Brasilia, designed by Oscar Niemeyer.

Double stair in a private residence designed by Charles Vandenhove in Namur, Belgium.

talented, free-thinking, left-wing young architect, Oscar Niemeyer, made that dream a reality? The young architect's personality was as exciting as it was controversial. What made him memorable from an architectural point of view was his hatred for Le Corbusier – who as an urban visionary would seem to have so much in common with Niemeyer. Now in his advanced and still fruitful career, Niemeyer still does not waste any opportunity to prove his predecessor wrong. As much of a rebel as a rival, he created one of the best-known staircase silhouettes of the post-war era for Brasilia's Itamaraty Palace (1958). With no handrail, no current safety regulations would have ever passed it. But it is technologically and architecturally magnificent – is it a

sculpture, a staircase or a visionary's variation on the intellectual theme of a staircase?

The National Assembly in Dacca, Bangladesh, by Louis I. Kahn (1962–74) was begun while the new city of Brasilia was still underway, but shows a different approach to public space. The central zone of the Assembly building comprises a complex of architectural elements which includes the staircase. Kahn's competence and knowledge in creating spaces speaks to the viewer better than any commentary. The system of marble lines delineating the individual pours of concrete into the timber shutters is symbolically an expression of human effort, and architecturally a design feature. The serenity of the entire building is maintained in the circulation space. What a shame that Kahn never saw the building finished. Staircases of the Modern

Movement – perhaps because of the conscious decision to re-define structural laws, to reduce the excess – are examples of splendid aesthetics and very often a remarkable (if sometimes very simple) level of craftsmanship.

So far, except for the earliest examples, this introduction has featured buildings designed by renowned architects. It is easy to forget that there are many examples of vernacular architecture by uncredited architects or builders that include ingenious and imaginative solutions to the problem of getting up and down. I was particularly drawn to the image illustrated here of a series of narrow apartment buildings in the Veneto region of Italy. The wooden outside staircases used to reach the individual apartments are certainly humble, but inventive and attractive all the same.

A well-worn mathematical formula can prove that compared with the number of possible

The central staircase of the National Assembly in Dacca, Bangladesh, by Louis I. Kahn (1962–74).

Simple wooden outside stairs attached to housing in the Veneto region of Italy.

variations for the future, a lottery bet is virtually a safe option. Looking at the staircases of the present and the very recent past shows how much history has changed and how much our lives have taken on a different dimension. The examples of historic stairs illustrated here show a great variety of approaches, ideas and executions but also their dependence on architectural styles and philosophies. Somehow everything was a bit tidier, more straightforward – uniting fashion, architecture, society, and life as whole. With post-war globalization, speed of communication, technological advances and scientific discoveries, everything is possible and almost anything is tolerated. This was not always the case. I vaguely remember my mother standing on the coffee table of her favourite dressmaker, who was adjusting the length of her skirts to what was then dictated by Paris fashion:

25 or 45 centimetres (9³/4 or 17¹/2 inches) from the floor was the strict rule regardless of the wearer's height. Similarly rigid dictates applied to the design of chair and table legs, or the lines of motorcars and washing machines. The birth of industrial fashion did not leave stairs untouched. Pre-fab houses and pre-fab stairs joined the family of mass production. Globalization does not seem to have narrowed the ever-growing range of staircase types now existing. In spite of high standards concerning people with disabilities, and high specifications as to performance and maintenance, designers, architects and artists are showing no limits to their creativity. Simply, there are fewer and fewer rules in the field of aesthetics, while the opposite is true in terms of health control and safety. Architects have grown used to

accepting different methods, different expressions, finding different ways of reaching the goal. Whatever the future might bring there is a very rich present to absorb, enjoy and admire. Even a complicated staircase represents a very small proportion of the overall investment involved in a total building. There is still a relatively large scope for architects to explore. The issue of the staircase might only be the salt added to the architectural stew, but without it there would be no flavour to speak of.

The following pages are not intended to provide a definitive survey of current staircase architecture, but simply present a personal choice of some of the most intriguing examples built in the last few years.

landscape staircases

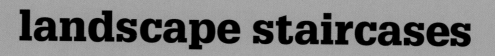

landscape staircases

There is a type of staircase which is closely associated with the landscape and which is designed either to blend in with the surrounding nature or to consciously create a contrast between the two. Very often these staircases provide an access to monuments or buildings. Sometimes their main function is to form a transition between the natural and the man-made, or the existing and the new, and their main design criteria and constraints differ from those which dictate the form and appearance of stairs inside the same buildings. In the majority of the examples chosen for this chapter the main characteristic remains the fact that they have no underside – they are either a part of a hill or literally form a hill. Being exposed to the elements they have to show resistance to the whims of nature and they have to be constructed in such a fashion that they will not be washed away by a sudden storm or flood. But all of this is invisible to the casual viewer, and for the designers or users just a matter of course. The aesthetics of the staircases have much more to do with their purpose and relationship with the object they are a part of. With a few exceptions they are considered, and function as, public spaces, surrounding an important venue or object, and as such they remain in our memories as part of the experience of that place. Think of the ancient monuments and medieval cathedrals illustrated in the preceding pages, or of more recently built theatres or big city financial institutions. Stairs of this nature, often filled with people eating their lunches and sunbathing, have become a significant feature of every large city. The buildings they belong to would not be the same if the stairs were taken away from them. As it was in the past, so it is now – the political importance of a building increases with a large public staircase surrounding it and the same could be said about its architectural impact. Every sculptor knows how important the pedestal is to his sculpture, every architect has experienced the struggle of marrying his building to the earth. A platform formed of steps makes the transition a little easier. The surface of the stairs is as much a means of communication as the basic form, since the material chosen for the staircase's construction not only creates a visual effect but also controls the details of construction. If we are not being visually distracted by too many other features, our attention to these details sharpens. There is an important transition – not only is the building a part of this game but the detail of junctions between the stairs and the landscape on the sides, top and bottom have their own role to play. Balustrading is only needed if the two surfaces part company and the danger of falling becomes a possibility.

Whenever you come across an external staircase which forms mainly an access, you will more than likely be astounded by a sense of overall strength conveyed with maximum simplicity. Both ancient monuments and those constructed in the recent past can be very similar in their appearance and use of materials, yet the monumentality is still not diminished by simplicity, which could be misunderstood as a lack of imagination. Concrete, plastic and other materials were introduced in the last century but have not stood up to the competition with their natural counterparts such as wood, stone or granite (glass has proved to be too slippery for external use). Possibly man is still intimidated by the endless variations manifested in nature and does not feel tempted to get involved in constantly lost battles, or perhaps there is not enough reason for the stairs to compete with either nature or the buildings they serve. With an increased interest in landscaping and city planning, a sense of public well-being has been resurrected. New technologies and contemporary ideas have found their way into both large landscaped projects and smaller endeavours, such as ramps and walkways carved into hills and slopes. While they are not exactly identical in scale, these smaller examples are an equally important means of overcoming differences in height.

The monumental timber staircase pedestal at the Bibliothèque nationale de France, Paris, by Dominique Perrault.

Atelier d'Architecture Chaix Morel et Associés / Musée Archeologique de Saint Romain en Gal / Vienne, France / 1995–6

This enormous archeological museum development is divided from the historic centre of the town by the Rhône River. The complex of buildings is totally free from any attempts to create a bridge between the past and the present. The building is constructed mainly of concrete and so are the staircases, forming a monumental access and simultaneously an integral part of an architectural concept. Interestingly enough, the homogeneous nature of the materials used for the stairs and buildings alike does not immediately communicate the hierarchy of individual design features, but rather finds its strength in the consistency of a total solution. The main stairs are constructed as a stepped concrete slab with minimum details and features, and form an entrance to this important public building that is both dignified and majestic in appearance.

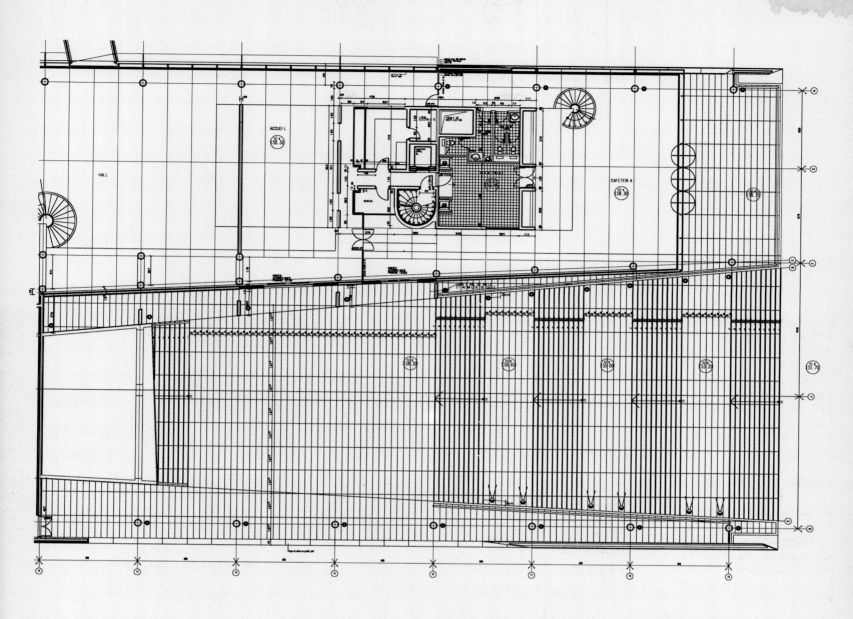

Opposite: When approached from the bottom, the staircase seems to meet the sky, not unlike many ancient monumental staircases of the past.

Above: The staircase's total area, shown in this plan, is as great as that of the building itself, underlining its role in the museum's overall concept.

There is an integral link between the building and the external staircase – neither would make much sense on its own.

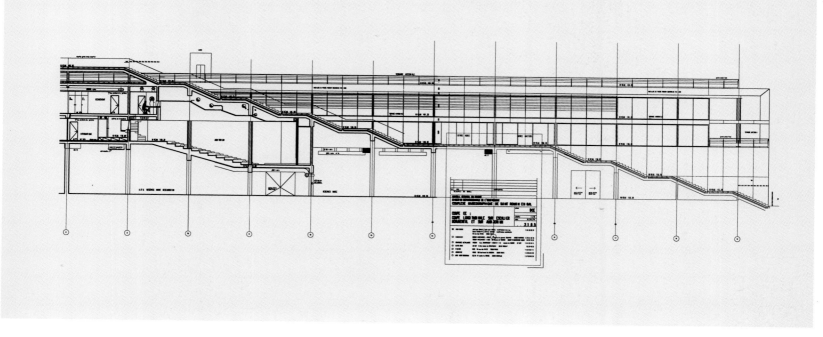

Top: Seen from across the river, the staircase's processional quality becomes even more apparent.

Above: The relationship between the form of the building and the staircase is clearly shown in the section.

Jose Antonio Martinez Lapeña, Elías Torres Tur, Miguel Usandizaga / Walkway at Castelldefels / Barcelona, Spain / 1990–93

The walkway leading to the castle at Castelldefels in Barcelona presents a very contemporary way of providing a new access to an old building. The problem of finding a democratic solution, equally suitable for those who are physically fit and those who are not, was resolved by a grandiose but almost brutal intervention resulting in a system of ramps stabilized by Cor-ten steel sheet piling with in situ cast concrete behind. The top of the steel formwork also serves as a balustrade – an obvious and strong protection to stop people from a quick and unplanned return to the bottom of the hill from which they started out. A bare landscape only accentuates the artist's intention to create an uncompromising statement.

**Opposite and above:
The sloping walkway
is stabilized by Cor-ten
steel sheet piling, which
is in turn supported by
cast concrete.**

The rough-and-ready quality of the corrugated, rust-coloured steel contrasts strikingly with the historic surroundings.

A bird's-eye view plan
shows the arrangement
of the steel pilings.

Bardají & Teixidor Associates /
Family Residence /
Colera, Spain /
1992–3

This access formed by stairs and a ramp attached to a private residential compound is a real attempt to find a sensitive approach to the landscape of the Catalan mountains around Girona. The residence (which consists of three houses for the various family members) was situated below street level to avoid protrusion into the landscape, and it is for this reason that the ramp was needed. The concrete structure is clad in stone, creating surfaces that are almost indistinguishable from the composition of the surrounding site. The ramp is also flanked by plants and trees to add to the natural effect. Certainly this is a modest and humble solution, but my obviously heretic and tough character prefers the brutal sheet piles of Castelldefels on the previous pages. (Mother, you tried so hard to bring me up as a nice gentle girl, I am so sorry!)

Opposite: A conscious attempt to blend in with the surrounding terrain, the steps and ramp are seen here against the backdrop of the mountains beyond.

Above: The retaining walls and the sloping surfaces create a strong composition. Strangely, both the ramp and the stairs direct the eyes to the distant horizon rather than towards the house, which is obviously not considered the most important player in this game.

The rugged effect of
the stones and mortar
in the retaining walls
is broken only by the
simplest balustrading.

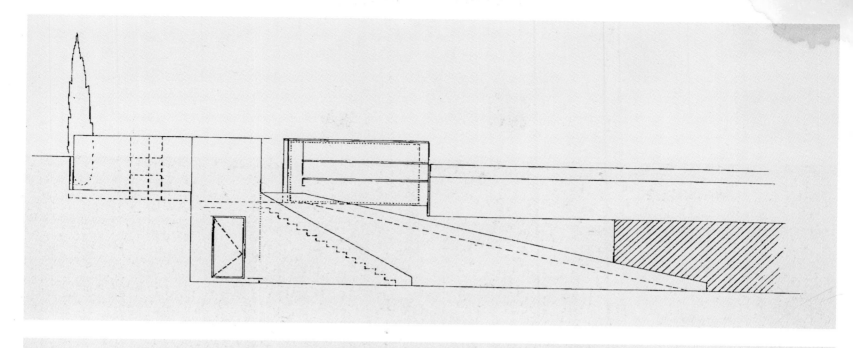

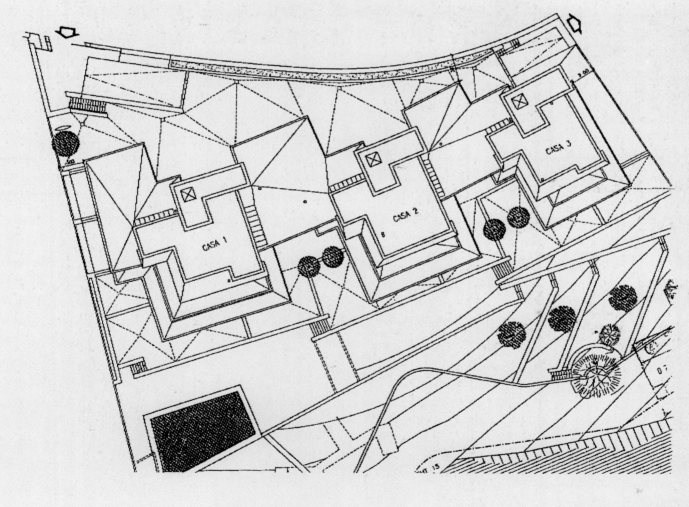

Top: A section through the terrain of the stairs and ramp.

Above: The ramp and stairs are shown at the top left of the site plan, which illustrates how the architects resolved a tricky compositional and topographical problem.

Antoine Predock/ Rosenthal Residence/ Manhattan Beach, California, USA/ 1993

The last example in this chapter takes us to a private house in Manhattan Beach, California. The house is designed as a somewhat unusual 'X' shape with an access to the upper level formed by exterior staircases, from which, depending on position, the visitor can enjoy views to Malibu, Palos Verdes and out to the Pacific. The upper level forms an almost independent platform towards which the individual flights of two independent staircases seem to lean. The symmetry and simplicity of the stairs underline the design intention – described by the architect as 'both a container and an object of delight' – and give the house a sense of importance and an adequate portion of monumentality. As mentioned before, the majority of stairs in the landscape do not seem to show their 'underwear', but this one certainly does. There is ever a rule without an exception.

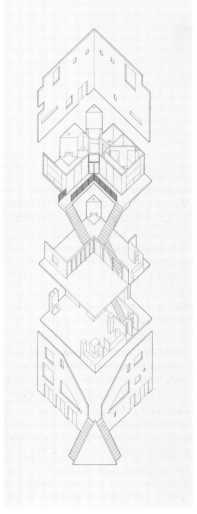

Opposite: The simplicity of the two repetitive staircase elements does not reduce, but rather enchances, the dramatic sculptural effect of the main entrance.

The inner courtyard on the second level continues the idea of the stairs meeting and parting in space – a space that is open but strictly defined.

An axonometric drawing explains how the three levels of the x-shaped house are all accessible from the outside.

Renzo Piano Building Workshop /
Cité Internationale /
Lyons, France /
1991–5

The Cité Internationale exhibition complex on the banks of the Rhône is an enormous project, of which the landscaped outdoor stairs form just one element. Not unusually, the stairs and their surroundings leading from the below-ground level entrances up to the adjacent landscaped park are clad in stone. In contrast, however, the buildings themselves are covered in terracotta and glass. The juxtaposition of these colours and textures is a theme that runs throughout the complex, but the main effect is one of a spacious composition that is soft and comfortable, does not intrude on the park, and above all is appropriate for the site.

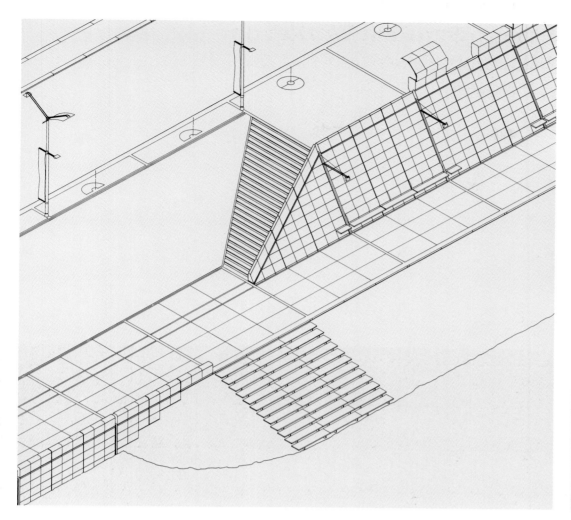

Opposite: The contrasting materials of the stairs (stone) and the adjacent building (terracotta) form a theme that runs throughout the project.

A drawing illustrates the transitions of the planes and slopes that lead down to the entrance level.

The completed result is harmonious and subtle – a testament to the skill, instinct and experience of the architect.

Dominique Perrault /
Bibliothèque nationale de France/
Paris, France /
1989–95

The new Bibliothèque nationale de France is one of the most important of the *grands projets*, the building programme that has had such an impact on the last quarter-century of French architecture. The transformation of a devastated industrial area on the banks of the Seine in east Paris has created an urban landmark and a meaningful public space. The perhaps questionable concept of enormous glass towers, to remind the visitor of four standing open books, is made even more grandiose by the formation of a vast stepped timber-clad platform – clearly an architectural attempt to design a pedestal for the monumental 'sculpture' of the towers. The symbolism of the project is easily legible through the clarity of the concept and the choice of materials. A transition between the past and the present, between the devastated and the recreated, between physical and spiritual, was achieved by the insertion of natural wood between the rough surface of the embankment and the lightweight nature of the glass towers. Unfortunately, the side effect to this splendid complex is extremely windy conditions. On the day I went visitors had to pay even humbler tribute to the architecture than they intended by slipping and crawling on the steps.

Opposite: The massive timber platform forms a pedestal for the four glass towers – a marriage of the natural and the artificial.

The stepped platform, called the 'belvedere' stairs because of the view it affords of the Seine, has become a popular public space in the summer months.

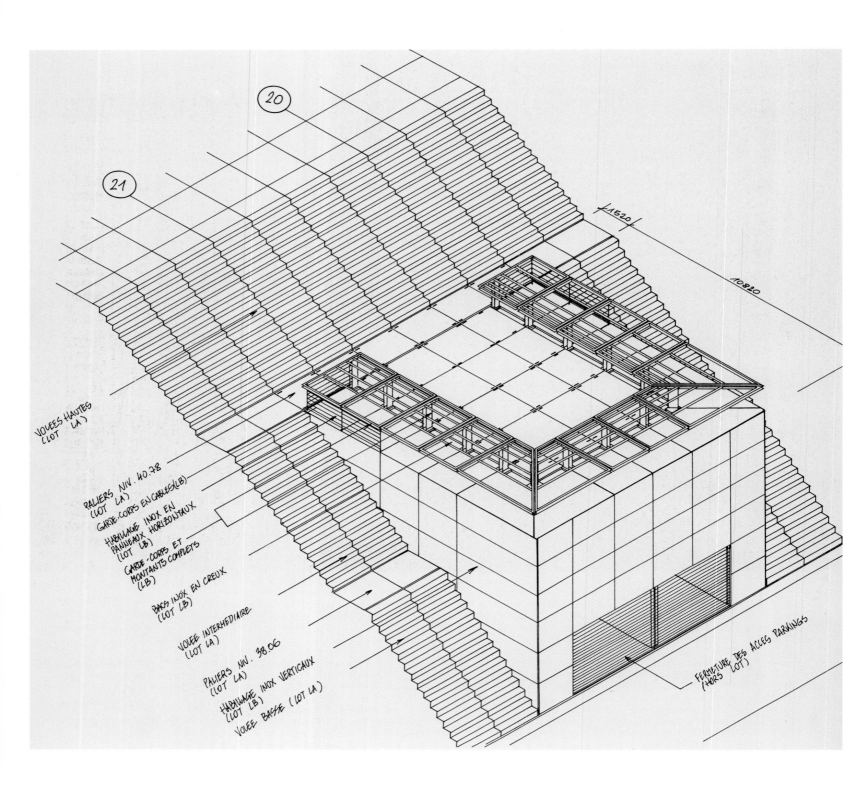

20

21

VOLEES HAUTES
(LOT LA)

PALIERS NIV. 40.78
(LOT LA)

GARDE-CORPS EN CABLES (LB)

HABILLAGE INOX EN
PANNEAUX HORIZONTAUX
(LOT LB)

GARDE-CORPS ET
MONTANTS COMPLETS
(LB)

BACS INOX EN CREUX
(LOT LB)

VOLEE INTERMEDIAIRE
(LOT LA)

PALIERS NIV. 38.06
(LOT LA)

HABILLAGE INOX VERTICAUX
(LOT LB)

VOLEE BASSE (LOT LA)

1520

10.820

FERMETURE DES ACCES PARKINGS
(HORS LOT)

**A drawing illustrates
how the bottom of
the stair platform
accommodates the
entrance to the
library's underground
parking garage.**

The contrast between
the earthy solidity of
the stairs and the airy
transparency of the
buildings is particularly
evident in this photograph.

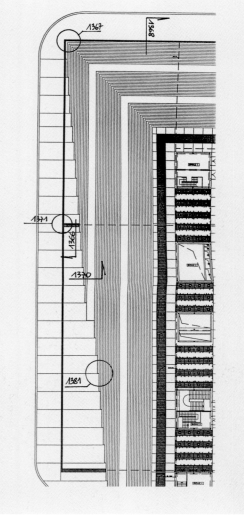

A plan of a corner of the
stepped platform where
it meets the street level.

glass staircases

glass staircases

According to Adolf Loos, a giant of the modern architectural era, all materials should be equal to both God and architects. This master died before Formica laminate, patterned with either stone or timber, was invented, and I am sure there is a range of other marvellous horrors – plastic mirrored bathroom tiles; textured, pigmented, decorated concrete panels with nicely embedded aggregates; linoleum in delicious pinks and appetizing greens – which would have made him think twice. But neither did Loos witness the incredible advances in glass technology, which makes me – I hope with his forgiveness – slightly amend the famous quotation: 'To God and architects, all materials are equal, with the exception of glass, which is more equal than others'. Tremendous progress was made in the 1930s as far as the use of glass in the building industry is concerned, including glazed façades, roofs, glass sculptures and bricks. Architects working between the two world wars dreamed about buildings clad in glass without any metal (with the exception of a few small-scale examples, this dream is yet to come true), but in spite of all the admirable courage to be found in that era of architectural history, it proved difficult to make staircases of glass where the glass would be acting as a structural element, rather than just as cladding, surface material or a decorative feature.

As we all know, glass is translucent or transparent, strong, plastic and easy to polish and cut. It can hold colour, it can be made to look colourful, it can be made relatively safe, it can be cleaned and easily maintained, it is hygienic and long-lasting. There is only one problem with it, as we also know – it breaks, and when it breaks it can hurt. We can make glass fire-resistant, bulletproof and shatterproof (laminated glass does not disintegrate when shattered), but we cannot stop it from breaking due to impact or to imperfections in the production process (which are very difficult to detect). Nevertheless, we know how to calculate the structural performance of a glass element,

whether it is fulfilling the role of a window, a panel in a glass façade or a stair tread. The fascination with glass is contagious and at one point practically caused an epidemic among architects, artists and engineers. Invention followed invention, innovation followed innovation. I remember entering an ideas competition in the 1970s for the Aspreys boutique, London, in which all the floors, walls and large curved display cabinets were to be made of glass. Of course I was not the first to think of it, but neither was it yet the time when the dream could be made reality. Feats that not so long ago seemed possible only in the imagination are now feasible in the realm of glass technology. With various technical processes the strength of glass has reached extraordinary limits and with the new possibilities comes the temptation to do more, go further. The first glass staircase I remember was in the Esprit clothes shop on the corner of Basil and Sloane streets in London, designed by Norman Foster. Glass was used as a simple sandblasted panel spanning two metal stringers. While admiring the skill of the design, I noticed a large piece of glass lying on the floor and an equally large chunk missing from one of the treads. The image of somebody standing on that very spot when the glass came loose and followed the laws of gravity is with me still. Nor will I ever forget the mirror on the fitting room door of the first shop I designed for Joseph. It was found by the cleaner early in the morning shortly after the shop's opening, on the floor and in precisely the same shape as when it had hung vertically on the door, but in a million tiny fragments. In this profession one needs as many guardian angels as there are available. Luckily our safety standards improve exponentially as our knowledge of glass increases. The collaboration between architects and engineers has never been so successful as in the examples included in this chapter. There are conservatories made entirely of glass, and there is a glass canopy by Tim Macfarlane, but we are

still waiting for a glass staircase that is not 'contaminated' by metal: what a challenge! Who will get there first? It is hard to fathom what entices architects into an obsession with glass over other materials. I know what led my practice to do our stairs, but I can only guess as to what motivates others. Appearance is of course an important factor, as are fashion, physical properties, structural potential and the challenge of technological innovation. And the inventiveness! The brilliance of ideas! Each project is a new story, a new experiment, a new discovery, a new achievement. In a way, it is another diamond fever – in appearance a diamond is not unlike a piece of beautifully polished clear glass, refracting like a prism. (The difference between these crystals is of course the price tag.) If I am to divulge our secret: the lure was a combination of two things. Firstly, we were fascinated by the structural potential of glass and wanted to stretch it to its limits – and we were lucky enough to work with a few ingenious structural engineers. Secondly, our overriding concern was how to get as much light through the building and to avoid creating dark areas (the space under a staircase is usually the most unattractive). It was a tremendous challenge to find yet another structural principle, a new solution, and – we hoped – not to copy ourselves. We wanted to see how far we could go and how many variations we could come up with. We have had a lot of fun – perhaps more so than our clients, who had to foot the bill. Many architects are in the race to prove that glass can eventually fulfil all their various dreams. If this is ever achieved, will it feel as great as we imagine? T.G. Masaryc said that 'the greatest gift to humankind is unfulfilled ideals. A dream come true loses its magic and challenge'. After all, an ideal fulfilled is no longer a dream.

'Floating' stairs in a Paris apartment designed by Guillaume Saalburg.

Eva Jiricna Architects /
Joan & David Shop /
Paris, France /
1994

I have designed glass staircases in many countries, including the United States, where building regulations are more stringent than anywhere else. So it was a great surprise to find out that a country with so many technically advanced buildings – from the Eiffel Tower to the Centre Pompidou – would not consider glass as a structural material unless it was specifically tested for each application and would not recognize toughened glass as suitable for balustrading. It is difficult to persuade a client to carry the expense of testing on a relatively small job, but in this case we had no other option. We won some of the arguments: the balustrading was declared safe, but unfortunately – even though all the test results were satisfactory – we had to support the glass treads with an element made of another material. We chose a folded metal plate reduced to the minimum possible size, which still allowed light to penetrate. The effect was somewhat unusual, so perhaps this requirement was lucky after all. Having had such a hard time with the authorities, I concluded that any challenge is good if it keeps designers on their toes.

**Opposite and above:
The stairs were hung
on a very light mesh of
horizontal and vertical
rods. When the shop
was later sold, the
pieces were dismantled
and easily transported
in a small van to their
new home.**

The distinctive metal
supports in the glass
treads came about as a
result of strict safety
regulations in France.

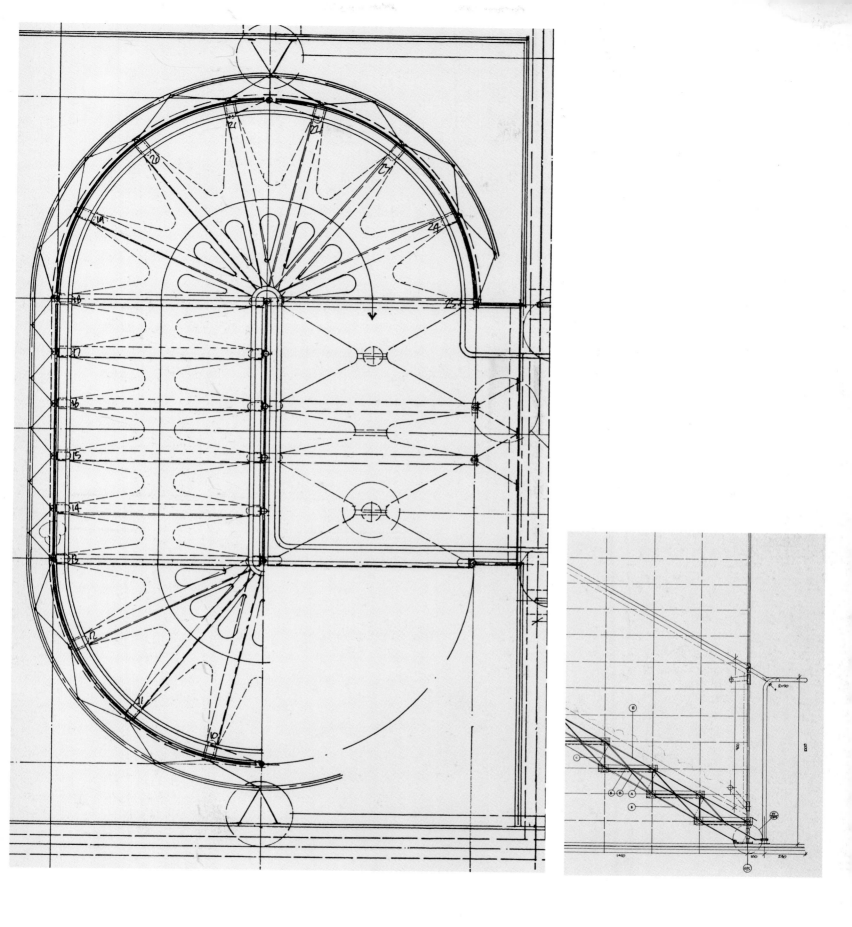

An overall plan of the staircase and first-floor landing, seen from above.

The section shows how the staircase was fixed to the mesh of metal rods.

Alan Power Architects–
Dewhurst Macfarlane /
House in Notting Hill /
London, UK /
1999

The staircase installed in this small terraced house in London's Notting Hill district could not have been built even a few years ago. The problem of securing the stability of the stairs in case one or more of the structural elements disintegrated could only be resolved by using laminated glass. In this particular case the glass is laminated to transparent acrylic panels. The main advantage of this brilliant proposal is how it increases the sense of space by distributing light throughout a potentially gloomy house. Of the main structural elements, the treads and one supporting wall are made of glass. The tripartite glass wall comprises acrylic panels sandwiched between toughened glass. The architects used transparent silicone tape and structural silicone to glue the glass risers and metal brackets together, a very brave solution. To prevent people from slipping on the stairs a series of sandblasted dots were applied parallel to the edges – the only translucent, as opposed to transparent, detail of the entire project. I have to congratulate the client for having selected such good architects and also congratulate the architect and the engineer for having been so imaginative and courageous.

Opposite: A solid wall on one side, a glass wall on the other, and a folded glass plane in between. What could be simpler?

The transparency of the stairs allows light to penetrate throughout the house, especially to the previously gloomy basement level.

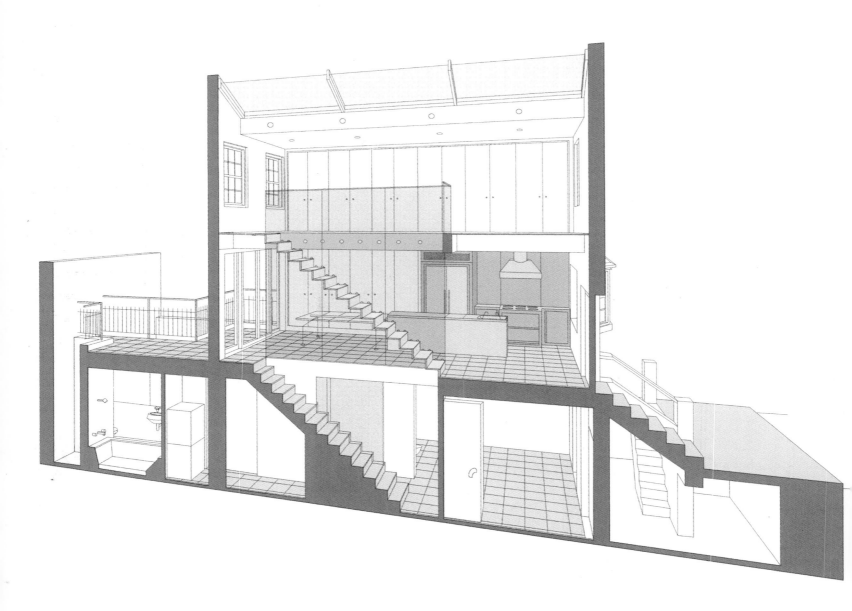

The section illustrates
the architect's aim to
open up the space in
the house so that light
could flow from front to
back and top to bottom.

Behind the façade of an ordinary Victorian house lies a sparkling architectural and structural jewel.

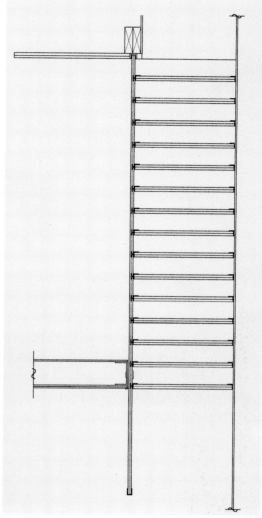

The front elevation of the staircase shows the solid wall on the left and the glass wall on the right. The latter actually comprises acrylic panels sandwiched between toughened glass.

James Carpenter Design Associates
– Dewhurst Macfarlane /
Tension Net Stair /
Chicago, USA /
1993–5

Given that two immensely capable people – the designer James Carpenter and the engineer Tim Macfarlane – worked together on this extraordinary staircase, the ingenuity of their statement is not surprising. Imagine that you are in the penthouse apartment of a 67-storey skyscraper in downtown Chicago and you are looking at this translucent structure consisting of a conical filigree core of stainless steel mesh (made of 4-mm [1/8-inch] diameter rods) and acid-etched laminated annealed glass treads. The central support is cleverly made rigid by a combination of very fine vertical rods and horizontal compression rings, and helped by the weight of the laminated glass treads and external cage of suspended balustrading. The internal and external structural elements are connected by aluminium rods which also support the treads. The use of stronger annealed glass has freed the treads from the normal constraints of four-sided supports or plastic back-up layers. This lack of extraneous supports contributes to the jewel-like quality of the stairs, and is also a great achievement in the field of glass structures.

Opposite: So minimal are its connections that the base of the stair seems to float above the floor.

A computer-generated view looking up at the stairs explains the structural concept and shows the meeting points of the materials and individual components.

The glass treads are supported by aluminium rods, which are in turn connected to the central tension net.

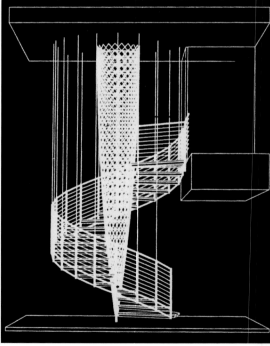

Above and right:
The lacy, delicate
appearance of the
tension net in these
computer renderings
belies its surprising
strength.

The treads are made of
stronger annealed
glass, which reduces
the amount of metal
supports needed.

Kengo Kuma & Associates /
Water Glass House /
Atami City, Japan /
1995

It is ironic that the design of this house, built as a guest villa for the maker of the Tamagotchi virtual pet, was influenced not by technology but by nature. The intention of the architects was to directly relate the glass box villa to the water surrounding it. The glass and steel staircase sits next to an artificial waterfall, and acts as a lighting device for the rest of the villa, as well as contributing to the villa's overall watery effect. Unlike the previous examples in this chapter, this is not a structural glass staircase, but rather a series of laminated glass treads supported by a steel truss, with low-visibility piano wire acting as a safety device to minimize the extent of the handrail. I am not familiar with Japanese building regulations, but I imagine it would be very difficult in a country so prone to earthquakes to create a total glass structure free of any support. In any case, from photographs of the villa it is obvious that the architect has achieved the desired water/glass effect of the project's title.

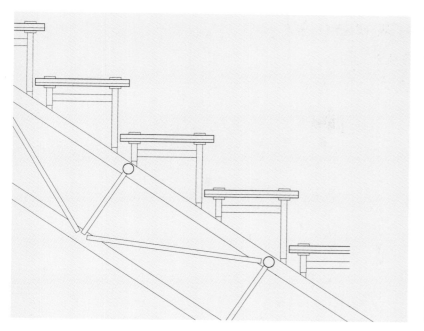

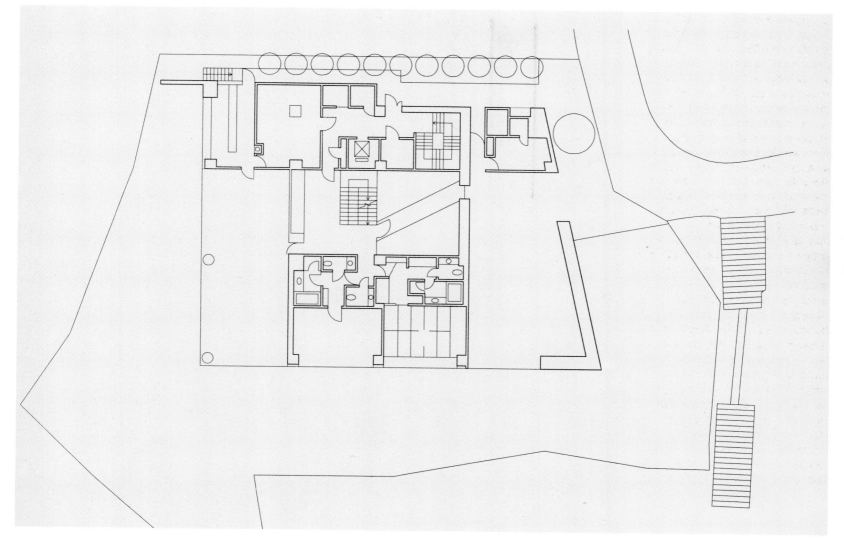

Opposite: The glass treads are supported by a substantial and rather complex metal undercarriage.

Top left: The section shows the depth and sturdiness of the frame, perhaps a safety requirement in a country prone to earthquakes.

Above: The second-floor plan of the house, with the glass staircase in the centre.

Top right: The second-floor landing, with a view out to the open atrium and bridge. The staircase echoes the house's theme of water and transparency.

Eva Jiricna Architects /
Joseph /
London, UK /
1989

The fashion retailer Joseph is one of our most visionary clients. With Joseph we learned how to work very fast, since in the retail trade a closed shop equals lost income. The Sloane Street shop has three levels and it is often difficult to make people circulate up and down without providing a 'magnet' to tempt them to explore. The magnet in our case was to be the staircase. It was to distribute daylight from the first floor to the basement, and it was to allow tantalizing glimpses of the treasures on display above and below. We set ourselves two tasks: to make the stairs as light as possible, and to make them easy (and therefore quick) to assemble. The final result was a Meccano-type of design consisting of small elements that could be put together quickly on site without complex scaffolding. Having designed a similar but smaller staircase in Joseph's nearby Fulham Road shop, we assumed this installation would be relatively straightforward. We learned, however, that to stabilize such a lightweight product on a much larger scale was not at all easy. When the shop was refitted a few years later, the stairs were dismantled and transported to a new home in Copenhagen, a task that proved much easier.

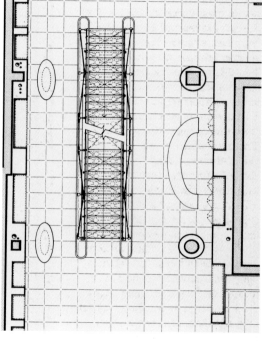

Opposite: Though it appears to be a totally flexible object, in reality the staircase is stable and allows hardly any movement in any direction.

The relatively narrow shop required a staircase that was as translucent and delicate as possible, in order to maintain a sense of space and light.

The ground-floor plan shows the positioning of this lightweight object within a solid box of walls, floors and ceilings.

The staircase was designed to be a magnet to shoppers, to allow enticing glimpses of the merchandise available on the upper and lower levels.

Detail of the metal
stringer. Bosses hold the
treads in position and a
bracing frame transfers
horizontal forces from
the handrail to the
stair's undercarriage.

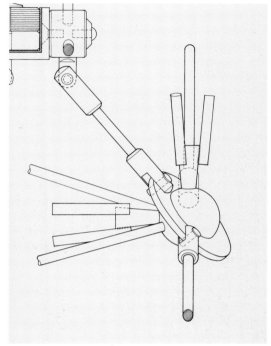

A drawing of the junction
of the structure's four
main components.

Guillaume Saalburg /
Private Apartment /
Paris, France /
1997

I have not visited this apartment, but I am lucky enough to have met the creator. He has a showroom and workshop on the outskirts of Paris and one of our friends – a builder – claims that this is where he would like to spend his holidays. What he really means is that the inventiveness and perfection of everything Saalburg does and displays in his showroom is extraordinary. Like the stairs in the Notting Hill house (see pages 52–5), the main structural elements are made of glass: vertical, suspended panels and horizontal treads that when viewed from the side appear to be floating in space. The architect does not reveal the secret of how he made the staircase, but he probably also used laminated glass, most likely glass laminated to glass rather than to acrylic. Because the treads look laminated to me, it is possible that he clamped them in a little 'shoe' on either side to avoid drilling. For structural reasons, the vertical panels are suspended and therefore avoid buckling when loaded. I can make an educated guess as to the technology, but the most important thing is to admire the result.

**Opposite and above:
The 'floating' staircase
comprises glass treads
held between two glass
walls, which are in turn
suspended from the
ceiling.**

Seen from the side, the glass treads appear to float, but this detail shows how they are in fact held in place by metal shoes, which are then screwed to metal straps on the other side of the glass wall.

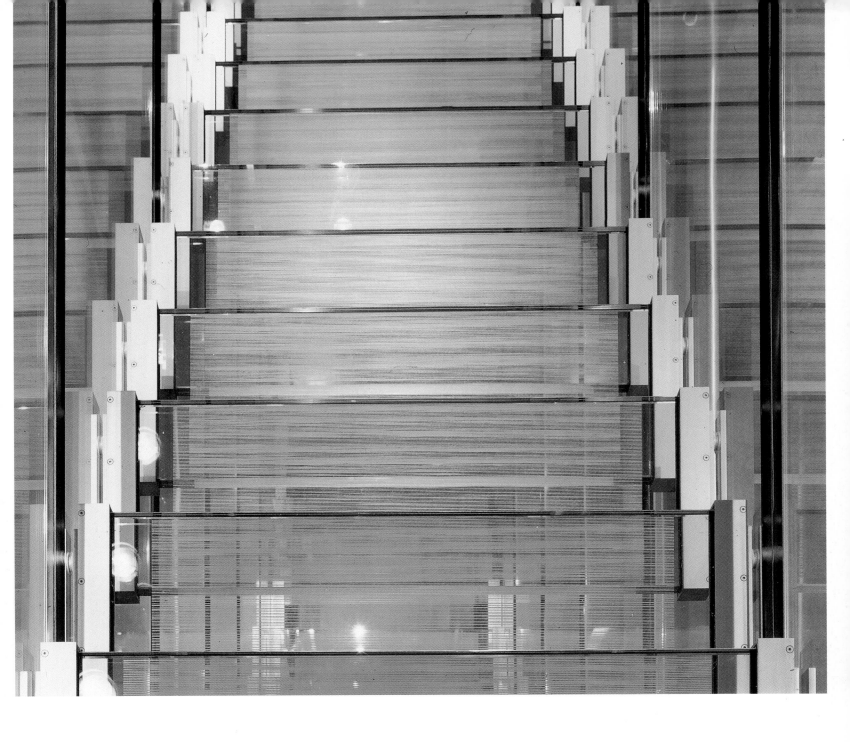

When seen from above
or below, the glass
treads are not
completely transparent,
but are in fact firelined,
a strengthening process.

nothing but the staircase

nothing but the staircase

Selecting staircases for this publication was a hard enough task; to then classify them according to their common denominators was much harder.

I found it rather fascinating to realize that some buildings are literally defined by their staircases, either because they occur in great numbers or because they overshadow the architecture of the building itself. On closer investigation a further distinction could be identified: either a project is a public building designed to accommodate a very large number of people, or it is the designer's intention to make the staircase the most important element, without which the building itself might lose its integrity.

Large theatrical performances or sporting events are not peculiar to modern times, nor are the problems of easy access and egress associated with them. The amphitheatres of ancient Greece and Rome still seem to be magnificently clever solutions. In the earliest examples, a naturally concave territorial formation provided the basic 'amphitheatre'. The 'stage' was the lowest point in the basin, and stepped sides functioned as both stairs and seating, for quick access and departure. Patience and discipline was not a typical feature of ancient crowds any more than it is of modern ones. In present-day theatres people still sit in the stepped arrangement of stalls and balconies, and

gain access via a variety of stairs, ramps and lifts. The theatre staircases illustrated in this book have been selected for their almost aggressive, overpowering presence.

Large shopping centres have been likened to cathedrals. People congregate in them, relax in them, even preach and fight in them. In my opinion they have more in common with large sports stadia. The main problem where a relatively large gathering takes place is dealing with the crowds who try to get out when the spectacle is over as quickly as they wanted to get in before it began. There were many means of access in the Coliseum at Rome, and they were all nicely hidden behind an impressive façade. A substantial number of present-day examples leave the staircases exposed. Is it simply a whim of fashion, is it the result of a more honest society trying to dispose of any camouflage, or is it simply a consequence of a level of conflict which makes people feel insecure about things that may be hidden? We are all aware of tragic events in the recent past concerning fires and crushes in nightclubs, football grounds and subway stations. Maybe the technology of the future will find a way to eliminate the dangers of vandalism, aggression and terrorism. Will such technology eliminate the types of buildings that have been a subject of this discussion? I hope not. There is something remarkably strong and memorable

about the examples illustrated in this chapter, and a great deal of architectural and engineering skill has been developed as an answer to these new conditions.

By contrast, there are a few examples here that do not seem to have any such negative connotations and which do not necessarily deal with large numbers. These are buildings in which the stairs act as such an important feature that the design statement as a whole cannot exist without them. Sometimes these stairs are symbolic and sometimes they are pure decoration (this is no negative comment – the time when my functionalist upbringing prevented me from accepting decoration as a possible alternative has long passed) and sometimes they are just the result of an architectural instinct.

Compare the ancient Greeks and Romans, fighting their way in and out of plays, with hordes of pop fans or football supporters sharing their moment of triumph or frustration as they shuffle out of modern stadia. Possibly the ratio between the instinctive and the rational in building design has changed and the technology developed by society moved on, but the role of staircases remains virtually untouched by it all.

The simple but repetetive staircases at the Kölnarena, Cologne, are the building's most notable feature.

Tadao Ando /
Japan Pavilion for Expo '92 /
Seville, Spain /
1990–92

The main staircase leading to the exhibition floor of Ando's Japan Pavilion has an almost ritualistic presence. In the tradition of ancient Japanese shrines, the staircase symbolizes the ascent into another world or experience. The form of Ando's staircase echoes that of the *taikobashi* – or drum-shaped bridge – and can be seen as a link between the West and the East. The unity between the material used for the building and for the staircase adds to the monumentality of the pavilion – in fact, it is the largest timber structure in the world. According to the architect, wood was chosen to convey the Japanese culture of naturalism to Europeans more accustomed to stone. Architectural drawings reveal the clever construction of the stairs, consisting of a pre-cambered beam tensioned by the cables of the handrail, symmetrically matched on the opposite side. Through the opening between the enormous timber structural columns there is a cheering glimpse of the sky. This very Japanese, and very emotional, statement typifies the talent of this architectural magician.

Opposite: The sheer scale of the project makes humans tiny by comparison – perhaps part of the symbolism behind the overall concept.

Above and right: The bowed shape of the staircase gives it the appearance of a bridge – according to the architect a bridge from East to West.

There is an escalator on
the left of the 'bridge'
for visitors unable to
climb the stairs, but
those who are able
may choose the more
arduous route as part
of the experience.

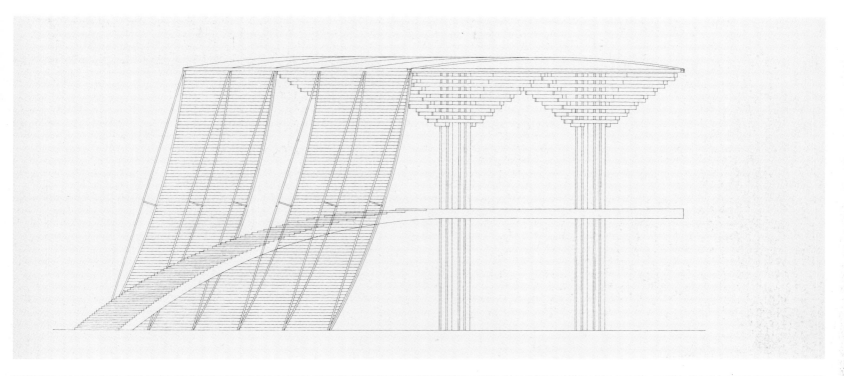

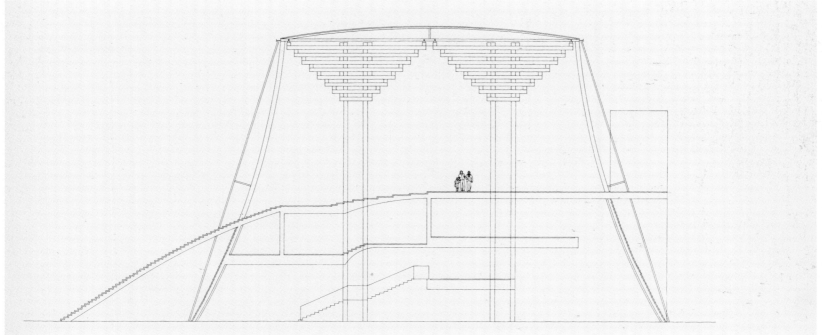

Top: The drawing highlights the juxtaposition of the concave curved walls and the convex drum-shaped bridge – both traditional Japanese characteristics.

Above: The section reveals how the bridge/staircase is not just a means of entry but also an integral part of the pavilion's main circulation space.

Joan Rodon /
Private house/
Collserola, Barcelona, Spain /
1995

Was the house built around the staircase or was the staircase built to suit the house? I was pleasantly surprised when the architect responded to my question by saying: '... the reinforced concrete staircase is the main element of the composition.' The staircase is more or less minimal, the private residence is more or less the opposite, but even in conceptual terms the simplicity of architectural elements prevails. What contributes to the richness is the selection of deep colours, certainly very appropriate for that part of the world. I cannot imagine that you would be allowed to fall into a blue mood, to get depressed or to cry if you were lucky enough to live in this house.

I wonder how a building inspector in the United States or Britain would view the absence of balustrading. Maybe Spanish children have several guardian angels, or perhaps they are just born with a better sense of balance.

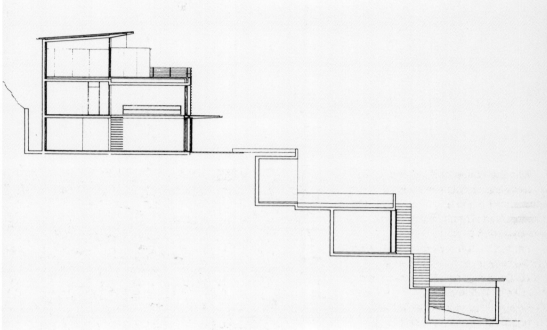

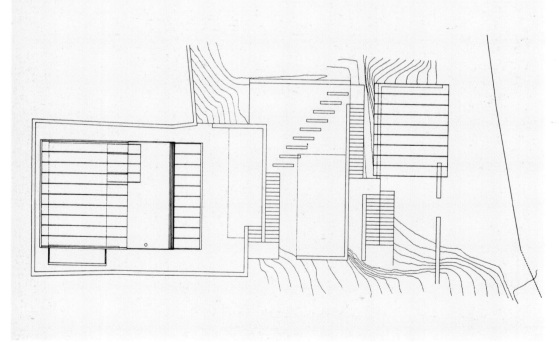

Opposite and top left: The house is built on the side of a hill. To reach the top visitors must negotiate a succession of steps and horizontal planes.

Above: The plan simplifies the many levels of steps and planes, making it difficult to fully appreciate the house's vertical complexity.

Top right: The section illustrates how the house itself is a series of steps up the hillside, which has certainly been reshaped and adjusted for this purpose.

**Above, top and right:
The house is a mixture
of colours and levels,
but the composition is
held together by the
unifying force of the
staircases.**

**Above: By attaching the
cantilevered stairs to the
sides of the house and
playing a game with solid
two-dimensional planes,
the architect has achieved
a three-dimensional effect.**

Schneider & Schumacher / KPMG Offices / Leipzig, Germany / 1996–8

For the architect designing the Leipzig headquarters of this international auditing firm, the main theme was transparency, for both environmental and symbolic reasons. The building's transparent outer skin not only allows daylight in, but leaves the circulation spaces, including the main staircase, visible from the outside. Free as it is from supporting walls, the staircase creates an interesting pattern and also allows light to pass from the outside through to the inner atrium. The stairs themselves are traditionally constructed of steel stringer and folded steel plate. One of the most striking effects is not structural at all. It is created by the red floor covering which continues from the walkways onto the stairs, and which is in vivid contrast with the grey of the rest of the building.

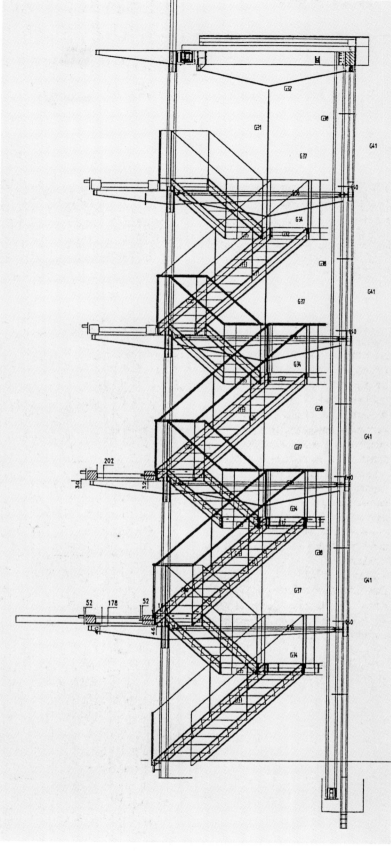

Opposite: Because the glass façade is distanced from the horizontal floor decks, the stairs seem to sit in a void, but also form a visual link between the glass skin and the solid core of the building.

Because the stair flights are separated from the floor slabs, the staircase's structure is very clearly expressed.

The section makes the somewhat unusual geometry more legible, and also reveals, on the right of the drawing, the suspension rod that stretches from the roof to the ground floor.

Above and opposite:
Though the construction
of the steel stairs is
traditional, a view
from above and an
architectural drawing
show that the geometry
is anything but.

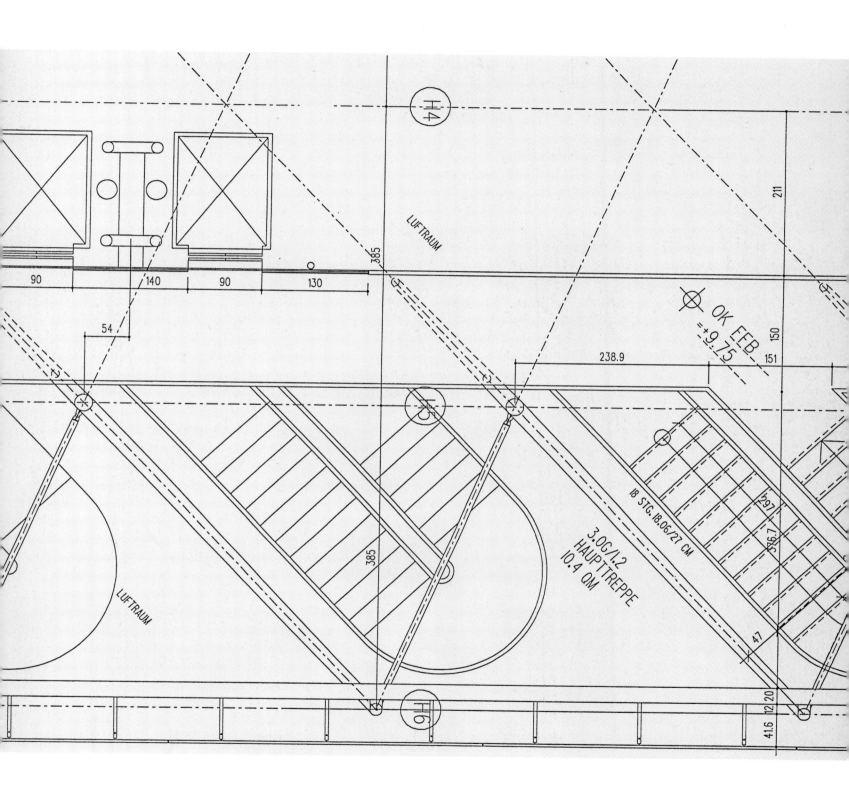

Pei Cobb Freed & Partners /
The Rock and Roll Hall of Fame
and Museum /
Cleveland, Ohio, USA /
1995

As dynamic as the music the building has been conceived for and devoted to, the central circulation space of the Rock and Roll Hall of Fame is full of bridges, stairs, walkways and terraces distributing people to various destinations. This sculptural arrangement animates the building and simultaneously creates the overall impression, the overall atmosphere of the place and its aesthetics. The juxtaposition of geometric forms, of the symmetrical and the asymmetrical, is intended by the architects to express the rhythm of rock and roll. The transparent balustrading allows for the joyful play of light and shadows and creates a feeling of lightness, allowing the visitors themselves to become engaged in a continual performance. The whole concept is about theatre, show and play.

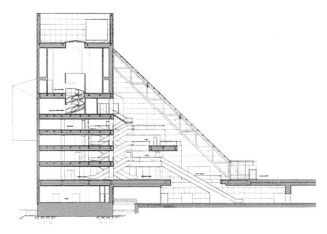

Opposite: Rather like the previous example, the bank of stairs and escalators creates an interior space between the main building and the glass atrium.

Above and right: The protruding stair at the top of the picture might seem like an aggressive attachment to the main structure, but for the people using it it offers a magnificent overview.

Top: A section showing how the stairs and escalators connect the building with the atrium. For people on the stairs the experience is somewhat like floating in space.

Riken Yamamoto & Field Shop / Saitama Prefectural University / Koshigaya, Japan / 1997–9

With curricula in nursing, social welfare and rehabilitation, Saitama University specializes in healthcare teaching and comprises individual departments with separate points of access and equally separate means of egress in case of emergency. The banks of staircases that define the rear elevation of the building link the study rooms and laboratories on the first floor with the other areas of the various departments on the upper floors. The simple staircase structure is defined on one side by horizontal floor decks projecting on the outside of the building, and on the other by the suspended landings to which the flights of stairs are attached. The stairs themselves function as a beam spanning between the landing and the building with a cleverly articulated edge detail. The simple frames of mesh balustrading that echo the stepped form of the stairs ensure that no objects can fall through and possibly injure anyone on the lower part of the stairs. Notice at the top of the staircase the clever triangle formed by the prop and the tie defining the end of the landing suspension cable.

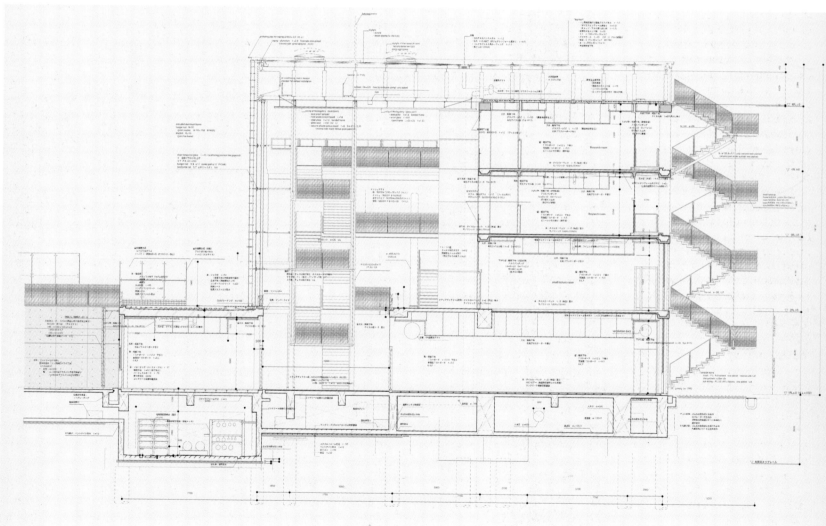

Opposite: The delicate detailing and elegant construction of the stringers make it easy to forget that the staircases are not just decorative but a serious safety requirement.

Top: The theme of stairs and fluidity between levels is carried on into the second-floor deck.

Above: A section through the building explains the relationship between the external stairs and the internal organization of spaces.

Axel Schultes Architekten /
Städtisches Kunstmuseum /
Bonn, Germany /
1992

The hour-glass shape of this staircase represents an extremely strong spatial concept. It is the nucleus of the whole building, connecting all the general parts of the museum – the foyer, café and bookshop, auditorium and toilets – with the exhibition spaces. It is made of Andeer granite from Switzerland, which makes a very soft transition between the floors, stairs and the walls. The handrail subtly denotes the limits of the extent of the stairs while the balustrading gently disappears into the surrounding context. The architects have modestly admitted their disappointment at having discovered that similar examples of this type of staircase have been previously constructed around Europe. Ideas are constantly appearing and disappearing in the flux of architectural history, and there will always be space for another revival. The talent of the architects is not diminished by the fact that they were not the first.

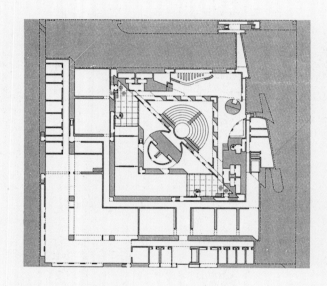

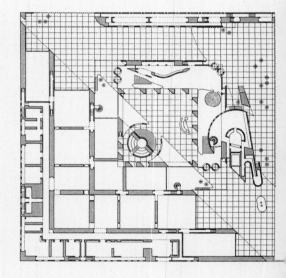

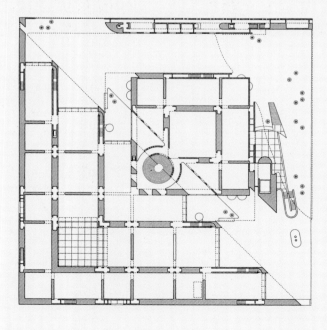

Opposite: Plans of the basement, ground and first floor (clockwise from top left) show how the central stairs form the literal heart of the museum, as well as providing the main circulation point.

The dramatic hourglass staircase gives the building its identity and provides the most memorable feature of the overall design concept.

Emmanuel Blamont and Lou Caroso /
Le Phénix Theatre /
Valenciennes, France /
1997

Designing a new theatre these days usually begins with calculating the number of fire escape stairs needed to ensure sufficient means of escape in an emergency. Such a requirement – and of course it is an appropriate one – does almost dictate the architecture of the interior spaces. By 'almost', I mean that it is the architect's choice whether or not to adopt the most straightforward solution. The architects of this theatre have evidently decided to do exactly that. Their approach is not technically or formally unusual. The one outstanding feature seems to be the dominant red colour. Otherwise there is a simple stringer, timber treads and powder-coated rods and tubes forming the balustrades. The strength of the solution lies in the repetition of the identical element. The impressive effect created by this jungle of individual parts and multiple features successfully overrides the everyday details and simple principles, and one can imagine how the effect is heightened when the stairs are crowded with theatregoers at the beginning and end of every performance.

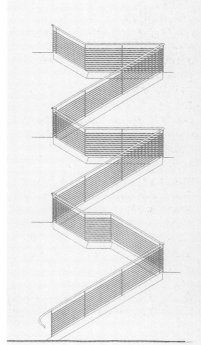

Opposite: The space between the two main zones of the building is devoted to moving people in and out of the main theatre.

Above and right: The structure and materials – metal balustrading and wooden treads – are not unusual. The striking effect is achieved through the use of vibrant red, eye-catching light fixtures and the repetition of a simple form.

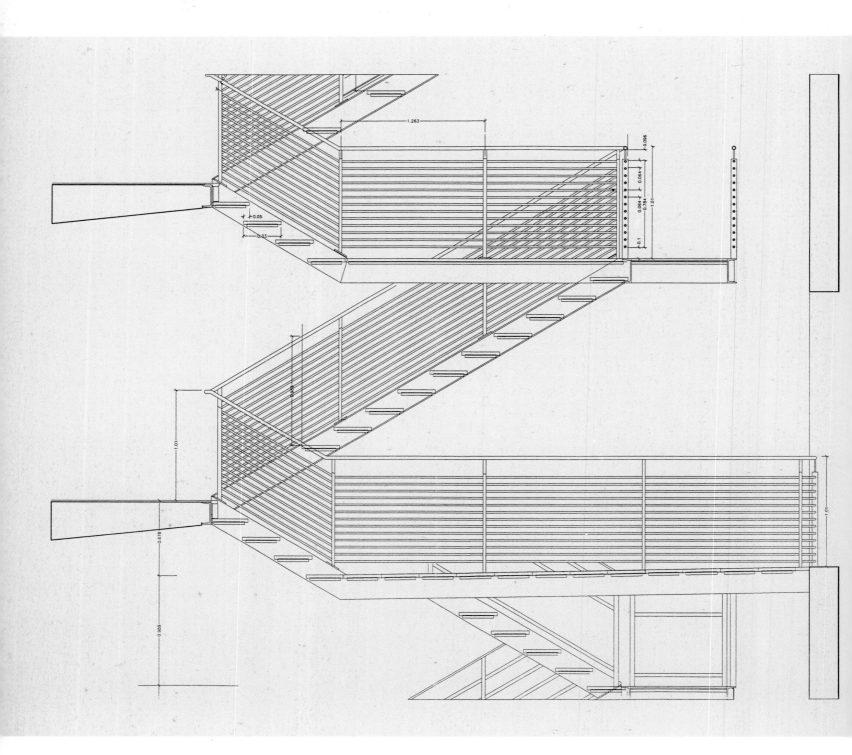

The drawing shows how the architects approached the problems of crowd movement and safety in the most straightforward way possible.

It is only when the
stairs and corridors are
full of theatregoers that
the space really comes
into its own.

Peter Böhm /
Kölnarena /
Cologne, Germany /
1998

The arena is recognizable from a distance by the enormous arch from which the roof is suspended. On closer observation you can see nothing but the stairs behind the glass wall and more or less the same view from a different angle when you enter the 18,000-seat stadium. It is hard to say which we fear most these days – fire, violence, panic, vandalism or terrorism. It is unfortunate that architects and their clients have to turn their minds to the most negative possibilities when designing public buildings and sports stadia. Remarkably, this particular example manages to maintain its design dignity within a very limited palette of materials and finishes. The overall concept is mainly monochromatic – perhaps this allows the colours of the fans' tee-shirts and caps to stand out more clearly. What would the builders of the Roman Coliseum think of the progress we have made since their time, apart from the obvious difference in the value placed on human safety?

Opposite: The entrance foyer is dominated by the banks of stairs that run around almost the entire stadium.

Safety concerns were a decisive factor in the choice of materials – concrete, glass and steel were chosen for their low fire-risk qualities.

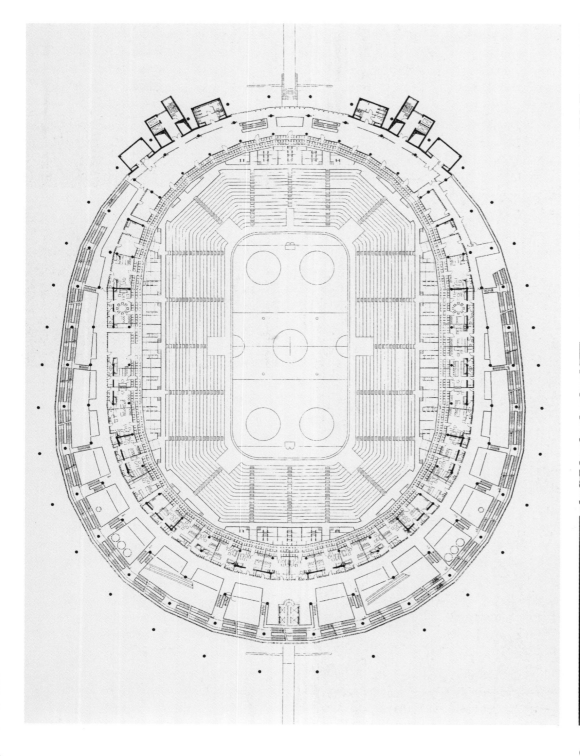

A ground plan shows the clearly expressed zone of stairs and associated circulation routes that encircle most of the stadium.

Concrete columns support a system of concrete beams, which carry the load of the landings and stairs. Metal balustrading allows views through the glazed envelope, following the overall concept of transparency.

Top and above: The simple glazed shell reflects the architect's concern that the building's elements should be clearly visible from both inside and out, night and day.

stairs as sculpture

stairs as sculpture

I think we can fairly confidently say that where there are people, there is Art. Consequently, if we can agree that architects are not to be excluded from this large family (forget your bad experiences), it should not be surprising to find Art in their creations, including staircases. There is a distinct general acceptance that Architecture is not synonymous with Building, and lots of controversial essays have been written on this subject without arriving at a definite conclusion. There will be no attempt here to prolong this particular polemic. My aim is simply to enjoy the fact that after so many examples of professional skill, technical expertise and technological tricks, there is a chapter full of wonderful attempts to change simple climbing or descending aids into remarkable statements, which leave no doubt in anybody's mind that an artist was present.

Even in early historic examples of staircases one can see a strong desire to go beyond the simple logic of what is purely functional, appropriate or essential, and to achieve a richer, more complex solution able to communicate much more than the simple transfer of body weight to higher or lower levels. The technology available to our predecessors might have been limited in comparison to what we have at our disposal, which gives our creativity more possibilities. On the other hand they had – rightly or wrongly – no restrictions on their design freedom, no regulations, no stringent safety requirements to stop them from doing exactly what they wanted or what somebody was willing to pay for (this last aspect is still as relevant as always). Sometimes it has to be

said that the discipline imposed by technology might clip the wings of even the most creative dream and only an adventurous designer will overcome or ignore the fear of potential failure.

It is a virtue of Art to question beliefs and potentially break down barriers; nothing is sacred to an artistic mind or pair of hands. Technical aspects are very often overshadowed by visual demands and creative aims. An affectionate kiss from the Muse is not guided by the 'rational' and not everybody will have the pleasure of being chosen. Nevertheless, those fortunate ones have been generous enough to share their wonderful experiences with us through their work even if such generosity may have resulted in jealousy or envy, and often unjustifiable criticism or mockery.
Having myself been born in the straitjacket of the dreaded architectural discipline, I can only admire the courage and skill of turning symmetry into asymmetry or complete disorder, using materials simply for their appearance rather than for their appropriate properties, forcing structure to obey aesthetic aspects rather than the laws of nature and being free to decorate without having to justify one's actions.

Recently architecture has opened up to new approaches, new interpretations, new constructions, which do not always belong to the categories of 'efficient', 'rational', 'economical' or even 'justifiable'. There is a new generation – or a re-born old generation – of designers, who, even a decade ago, would not have had a chance to enrich our culture with their revolutionary approaches to everyday problems. Suddenly everything is

possible, we are willing to expand our horizons. So what happened to all the rules, restrictions and limitations? Inventiveness has no limits. There is more concern than ever, thankfully, for those who are disabled or otherwise incapable of using stairs; elevators and other appropriate devices have made enormous progress even if there is still a long way to go before we reach the point where elevators for the disabled display the same level of artistic skill as stairs.

It is refreshing to see how many architects have recently used their imagination to introduce aesthetically pleasing graphics to reduce the hazard of public stairs for people with visual impairments. There is always a new way of looking at an old problem, and equally, there are strong solutions to look at, to admire and to follow.

In some examples in this chapter the staircase is an integral part of the spatial creation while in other examples stairs are woven as sculptures into the existing spatial formation. There are staircases designed to carry artistic applications, there are artistic decorations applied to staircases. There is a richness of ideas and interpretation, there is a richness of skill. I have an endless admiration for technology, structure and inventiveness – I also have an enormous admiration for artistic talent. Is it possible to say which is more powerful? Maybe it is better not to look for an answer and just enjoy the choices.

The unusual 'bird's nest' staircase at the German Parliament in Bonn, by Behnisch & Partner.

I.M. Pei & Partners /
Pyramide du Grand Louvre /
Paris, France /
1989

There cannot be many buildings which have provoked as many architectural and public debates as the Louvre pyramid. In spite of the controversy, as is so often the case, it has now become part of the country's heritage. This large glass jewel in the middle of historic Paris has been totally accepted, and nobody will ever discuss again whether this, the gesture of an ambitious politician, was appropriate or not. In the architect's summary a complex explanation is given as to the urban, architectural and practical concepts, without a single sentence devoted to the significant feature of a spiral staircase leading down from the level of the main court to the new entrance hall. An elegant spiral supports the steps without any interruption, whilst gently winding towards the main public circulation space. There is an uninterrupted view through and above a glass balustrade, finished by the simple line of a handrail. There are many examples of spiral staircases that are engineering miracles or architectural monuments. This one joins the family not perhaps for its technical merits (even if it is a pretty magnificent example) but mainly for the role its composition, proportion and scale play in the entrance space.

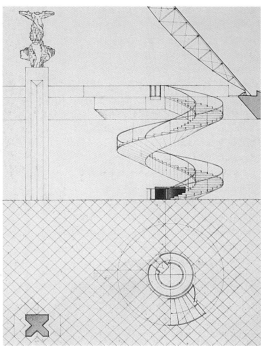

Opposite: An unusual view up through the spiral staircase that leads from the Grande Pyramide to the entrance hall below.

Above and right: The staircase appears to be an elegant ribbon, and the illusion is increased by the nearly invisible glass balustrade.

The smooth metal underside and simple glass balustrading contrast markedly with the complex scaffolding of the pyramid above.

The top of the staircase provides a sort of transitional observation deck from which visitors can view both the old Louvre courtyard above and the ultra-modern entrance hall below.

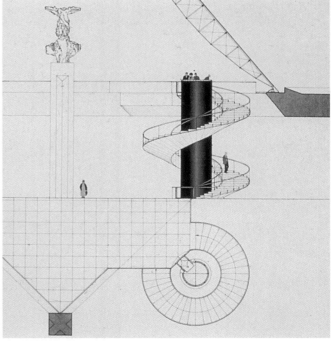

As this architectural drawing illustrates, the spiral undergoes a transformation when the central elevator platform is raised to the upper level.

Stefanie Zoche /
Maastunnel 'Sleeper' Installation /
Rotterdam, The Netherlands /
1998

However grateful we might be to technology for having provided us with various mechanical means of vertical movement, many of us find ourselves equally disappointed by their design qualities and aesthetics. As a rule, modern escalators and elevators are purely commercial objects without anything exciting to offer. However, since it is generally the architects who specify elevators, travellators and escalators for their new buildings, they have been known to carry out 'design improvements'. Look at the escalators inside Richard Rogers' Lloyds building in London with its exposed wheels and rails, or any new architecturally conscious development that tries desperately to 'civilize' a standard catalogue product. Stefanie Zoche, a fine artist, was obviously occupied by the same concern and came up with her personal solution. If you are lucky enough to travel up the escalators of the Maastunnel in Rotterdam, you will see 28 portraits of sleeping men and women. I am not sure how easy it would be to enjoy this installation during a busy rush hour, but when the escalators are empty they look great, and as an attempt to bring our attention to an everyday product it does the job. Manufacturers should take note.

Opposite: The risers of the escalators display 28 portraits, the subjects of which all appear to be sleeping. The theme of sleeping could be seen as a comment on the self-absorption and isolation that people often experience in cities.

Because the portraits are constantly moving, each passenger can enjoy a slightly different visual experience.

Philippe Starck / Restaurant Theatron / Mexico City, Mexico / 1985

No one has influenced recent architecture and design and their commercial aspects more than the extraordinary Philippe Starck. His imagination and competence, combined with an intuitive flair for business, began to make waves in the field of the industrial design, and then moved into interior design, architecture, product and exhibition design. His collaboration with the American hotel entrepreneur Ian Schrager has only added to Starck's success as an international interior designer. The dramatic entrance staircase has long been an important factor in Starck's interior designs, and the name of the project illustrated here – Theatron – says it all. Do not be confused by the image – all you are looking at is the entrance to the bar/restaurant. The scale and the spatial grandiosity of this project, which serves a relatively unimportant public function, would not be out of place at the Paris Opera. Is the armchair dramatically perched on the stairs waiting for you, or for someone equally famous? This is not important. The fact that you are a part of the scene makes you feel special, as if you have just actively participated in the creation of a work of Art (although, as photographs never seem to show people on the stairs, perhaps the magic disappears in the presence of an ordinary soul).

Opposite: The entrance staircase has something of the grand scale of cathedral steps. Structurally, however, the stairs are relatively simple – just a series of timber treads and risers.

The surroundings contribute to the impression that the stairs are a stage – curtains, spotlights, a large framed portrait – while the armchair on the landing is a mini stage set in itself.

Pei Cobb Freed & Partners /
Main Public Library /
San Francisco, USA /
1992–6

The Main Public Library in San Francisco represents American architecture of the last decade as much as it represents the attitude of a city that invested in a building of such an important public nature. An enormous complex of functions is organized around an atrium with a large skylight which not only brings light into the very heart of this vast volume, but also helps the visitors to understand their position in space. The role of the staircase here is not unlike that of Pei Cobb Freed's Rock and Roll Hall of Fame (see pages 86–7). There is a glass elevator, as you find in many other American buildings, and there is a large staircase woven into the walls of the atrium, which fulfils the role of a large viewing platform, thus involving the users in an intimate connection with the library. It is a definite attempt to create a three-dimensional feature in the overall design of the central atrium – a sculptural contribution to a public interior.

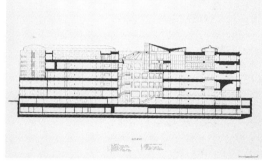

Opposite: The role of the staircase as a focal point is emphasized by the fact that it wraps around one of the library's four integral artworks.

As the staircase reaches the top of the building it wraps around a sculptural set of complex concrete elements.

Above and top: The atrium links the different departments of the building. Within this the staircase plays an important role by providing a vertical circulation element that also acts as a viewing platform.

Peter Zumthor / Thermalbad / Vals, Switzerland / 1990–96

The Thermalbad building is set into the side of a mountain, and to increase the feeling of having been carved out of that mountain local stone was used. In terms of creating an atmosphere of relaxation, mystery, and spirituality, this building is a masterpiece. Working with the contrast between light and dark, reflections in the water and the eerie disappearance of form in a mist of steam creates a truly memorable environment. The composition of the walls, ceiling and stairs – which allow shafts of sunlight through the slots of the ceiling blocks – combined with the tremendous discipline of the design elements (proportion, hierarchy of forms and control of light), gives the impression of permanence and continuity. The circulation areas, including the staircases, are based on a system of layered planes to create a continuous, flowing space. There is no bad or complex detailing, nothing which does not belong.

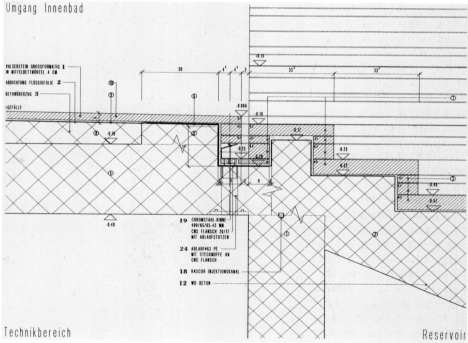

Umgang Innenbad

VALSERSTEIN GROSSFORMATIG **1**
IN MITTELBETTMÖRTEL 4 CM

ABDICHTUNG FLÜSSIGFOLIE **2**

BETONÜBERZUG **3**

>GEFÄLLE

19 CHROMSTAHL-RINNE
    400/65/65-43 MM
    CNS FLANSCH 20/17
    MIT ABLAUFSTUTZEN

24 ABLAUF#63 PE
    MIT STECKMUFFE AN
    CNS FLANSCH

18 RASCOR INJEKTIONSKANAL

12 WD BETON

Technikbereich   Reservoir

Opposite: The walls and stairs are formed from the same stone, lending all the structural elements an equal sense of importance.

The shallow steps leading to the Turkish baths do not represent a separate zone, but instead reflect the architect's intention to create a continuous, flowing space.

Not all the stairs in the building are above water: this section shows the construction of stone steps leading into the indoor pool.

Joan Rodon /
Castle of la Geltrú /
Vilanova i la Geltrú, Spain /
1994–5

Built as a fortress in the thirteenth century, the castle of Geltrú has been remodelled numerous times, and now houses the district archives. The original courtyard staircase was introduced in the fifteenth century, when it was decided to dedicate the ground floor to animals and the upper floors to human residents. As would be expected from an architectural feature of this period, the stonework was richly decorated and partly covered by a porch. Joan Rodon makes no attempt to recreate the previous glamour with his new staircase. It is simple and unpretentious, carrying the memory of the past without re-inventing lost and forgotten details. By using stone, the reference to the original concept is clearly legible even if only two pierced roundels and one small carved dog are included as a reminder of the richness of the past. The simplicity of the solution is sensitive and elegant and mercifully free of pastiche.

There is a very clear cut division between the old and the new, and no competition between the two. This is an example of discipline and modesty in the right place.

Opposite and above: The addition of a new staircase to this old fortress was a sensitive issue, but remarkable simplicity and attention to detail makes the new statement blend in very easily with the existing fabric of the building.

**Opposite: The architect
has not attempted to
recreate the elaborate
stonework of the
original staircase,
although a carved
dog at the end of the
balustrade serves as
a playful reminder.**

**The section shows
the placement of the
staircase within
the courtyard.**

Coop Himmelb(l)au /
Groninger Museum /
Groningen, The Netherlands /
1993–4

The East Pavilion of the Groninger Museum houses art from the sixteenth century to the present. The museum was designed by Studio Mendini with Coop Himmelb(l)au as guest architects. Coop Himmelb(l)au's design for the pavilion's rooftop gallery tries to establish different levels at which the collections on display can be experienced, as well as to vary the levels of circulation. For this reason an outdoor staircase connects the levels with Mendini's ground-floor gallery. The design process involved a very complex system of layering three-dimensional studies with the original sketch designs, creating a sketch model and then enlarging it digitally to the actual scale. This was consequently realized by using local methods of shipbuilding to construct the primary elements such as the prefabricated steel plates, which were produced ready-to-fit, complete with insulation, paint and rust-effect detailing. The jagged profile of the metal staircase, painted the same red as the panels, nicely echoes the 'exploded' appearance of the building.

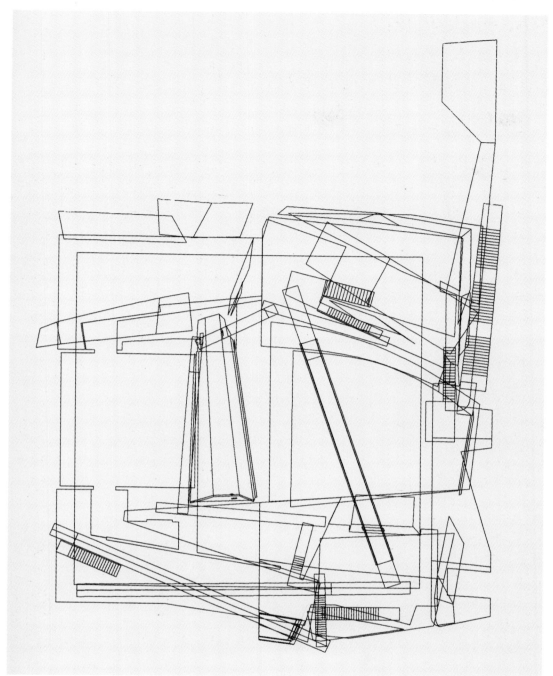

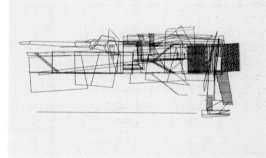

Opposite: The main external staircase is painted red to match the 'rusty' metal plates behind, while its rather jagged profile echoes the chaotic, exploded forms of the gallery.

Because of the gallery's complex structure the plan is not easy to understand, but the external staircase is clearly identifiable at the upper right of the drawing.

A concept elevation drawing showing the staircase on the right, leading to the gallery entrance.

Antoine Predock /
Central Library and Children's Museum /
Las Vegas, USA /
1990

The most remarkable aspect of the Children's Museum must be the Mad Scientist's Tower (as the architect refers to it). The triangular space – filled with individual stair flights and appropriate landings – is dramatic, slightly scary and yet playful at the same time, and certainly creates the kind of magic so closely associated with a child's imagination. In terms of materials and finishes – concrete and metal – there is hardly any richness to speak of, and yet the result is wonderfully complex, interesting and meaningful. What is not expressed through forms and materials is achieved through lighting – both natural and artificial. From the tower's summit one can admire the city of Las Vegas and the surrounding mountains. Visitors who reach the top can also stand on the glass platform and look down the triangular stairwell – a thrilling, if vertiginous, view.

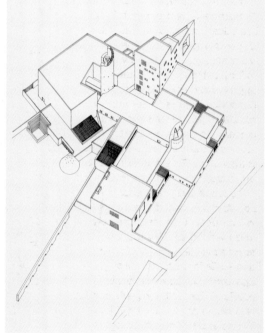

Opposite: A view up the stairwell to the triangular skylight at the top. Landings are formed at the points where the straight flights are attached to the sides of the round tower.

A glazed opening at the top of the stairs allows visitors to stand over the open space and enjoy the vertiginous view down. The vibrant red floor increases the sense of drama.

Top: The materials and colours are low-key; it is the geometry and lighting that create the effect.

Above: The Mad Scientist's Tower is near the top left of this axonometric drawing.

Ricardo Porro and Renaud de la Noue /
Collège Fabien /
Montreuil, France /
1993

Ricardo Porro – a philosopher, architect and artist – creates, designs and builds in an extraordinary manner. I have selected this project on the basis of my admiration for Porro and de la Noue's amazing ability to sculpturally interpret a relatively common space – the entrance to a junior high school. I was impressed by the form of the staircase, which produces remarkable effects within the interior of the entrance hall. The architects describe their intentions eloquently: 'This is the central stairwell of the building and it is an important element of the meaning of the architecture. Its shape is not only sculptural, it corresponds to the idea of "continuous space and time", a fundamental question of art and science in the twentieth century.' They go on to say that this idea had already been explored by artists such as Marcel Duchamp with *Nude Descending a Staircase*, Pablo Picasso in his Cubist paintings, and even Salvador Dalí with his liquid watches. 'We have expressed in the entrance hall of this high school the notion that multiple movements can be captured simultaneously.'

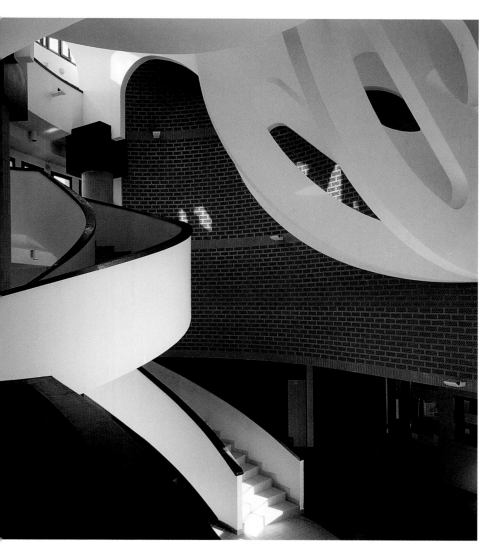

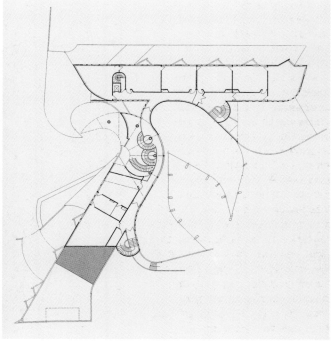

Opposite: By creating this undulating double-spiral the architects sought to express the idea of continuous space and movement.

To increase the sense of movement, the architects have incorporated other sculptural elements, while stained glass windows provide changing coloured light effects.

The staircase appears in the centre of this third-floor plan. The concrete spirals are cantilevered out from the suspended footbridge that connects the two wings of the building.

Ron Arad /
Tel Aviv Opera House Foyer /
Tel Aviv, Israel /
1989–94

I remember Ron Arad from the very beginning of his artistic career, when he started experimenting with car seats and turning them into armchairs for people's living rooms. During the High-tech era of the 1980s it was neither strange nor extraordinary. What is truly extraordinary is the development of his creativity ever since. Having just visited his exhibition at the Victoria & Albert Museum in London I can only admire his endless potential as an architect, engineer, designer and artist. He no longer needs car seats to 'dress up' or down – he designs chairs in any shape and material and, more importantly, you can sit in them. There is no doubt in my mind that what he does is Art. The fact that the Art is also functional is a bonus. This principle applies to the bronze staircase at the Tel Aviv Opera House. It is without doubt a sculpture – the whole space is a sculpture. There is wit, and there is discipline. The richness of forms and materials, and the quality of the product and the detailing are all proof that a great artist was in charge.

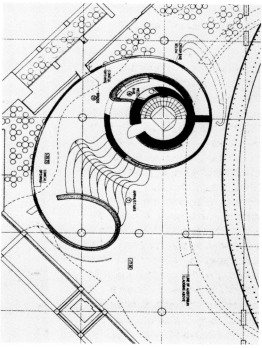

Opposite: The bronze mezzanine staircase is yet another example of the way in which Arad skillfully expresses form in polished metal.

The designs for the foyer were conceived as a series of flowing, free-standing forms, or 'islands', which could interact with each other.

A plan shows how the staircase forms part of a shell-shaped island structure that incorporates the mezzanine-level amphitheatre (the circle at the top of the drawing) used for foyer performances.

Ron Arad /
Diego Della Valle Offices/
Civitanova Marche, Italy/
1999

As opposed to the Tel Aviv Opera foyer, which is a totally spatial solution (staircase included), the staircase for the offices of the Diego Della Valle fashion company is a free-standing sculpture in space. It clearly carries the design features for which Ron is so famous in his furniture design. Giving the impression of a sea shell that hides an amorphous creature within, it is an extremely competent statement – very strong, and very comfortable with its surroundings. The brightly polished stainless steel body, made to an extraordinary degree of perfection, reflects not only the light, but also everything around it. It acts as a mirror, with a mirror's wonderful capacity to add extra depth, to extend the sense of space. There is no intention to create a drama; the drama simply follows as a natural consequence of the concept and its realization. The ambiguity of the inside versus outside is remarkably successful. It is a piece of Art in the right place and as such it fulfils its role perfectly.

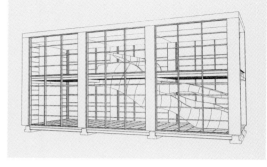

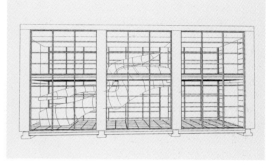

Opposite: Visitors come out of the top of the staircase as if emerging from an open mollusc.

When seen from the back, the ground-floor entrance to the staircase appears to be some sort of sculpture suspended from the ceiling.

Top and centre right: The architectural drawings illustrate the staircase's role as a single sculptural object that pierces the first-floor level.

Above: The back of the first-floor entrance: the highly polished, stainless steel surface acts as a mirror, adding depth to the space.

Behnisch & Partner/ German Parliament/ Bonn, Germany/ 1992

Two of the staircases in this building are featured here. The first is the wide, ramp-like foyer staircase. It is appropriately monumental, and at the same time conveys the sense of simplicity, space and openness that the architects sought to create. The other staircase, known as the 'bird's nest', is situated next to the assembly hall and is surrounded by an intriguingly complex sculptural composition in timber, which forms the balustrade. What fascinates me in this particular example is the overpowering desire to achieve a complex result based on a very simple structural and architectural concept. Why was such an overwhelming complexity required or desired? The architects explain: 'Objects and areas should tend to be unfettered; they should be able to develop in accordance with their own laws. They should assume their roles in the overall structure, but beyond that they should be free.' Perhaps this is the architects' comment on the nature of democracy.

Opposite: The stone entrance staircase brings visitors into the foyer. The glass balustrading panels echo the building's overall theme of light and transparency.

The ordinary metal stringers and timber treads are rendered extraordinary by the complex timber structure that forms the balustrading.

From the 'bird's nest' staircase visitors can watch proceedings in the glass-enclosed plenary chamber.

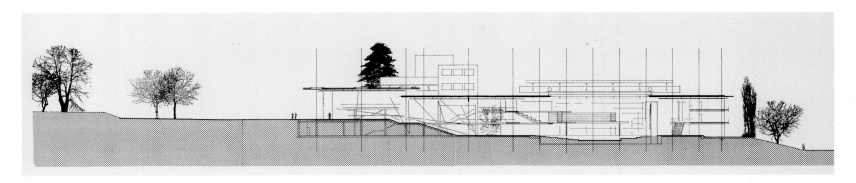

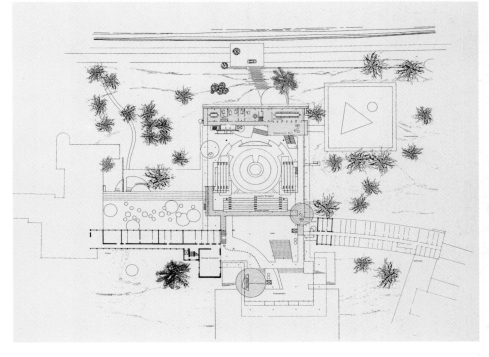

Top: Section showing the two staircases near the centre.

Above: Floor plan showing the foyer staircase at the bottom and the 'bird's nest' at the top right of the building.

technical staircases

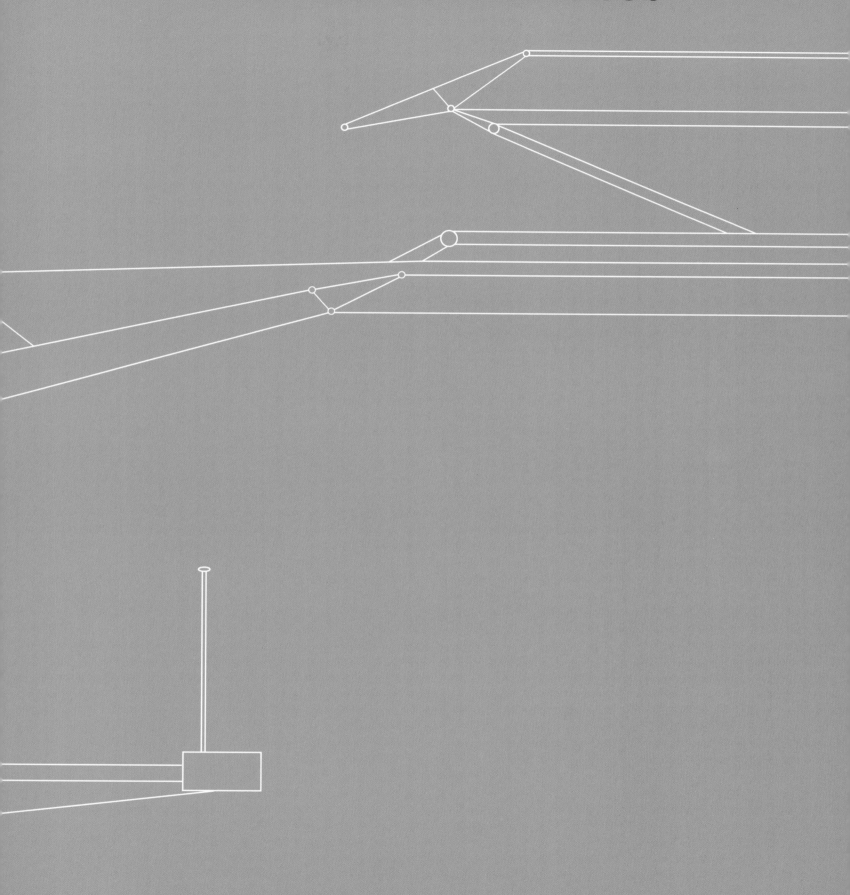

technical staircases

Like any other element of a building, a staircase is both part of a structure and a structure in its own right, and its basic principles have to obey structural laws. Whether this awareness of the structural performance of a staircase – or any other part of a building – is expressed by the architect or not is a matter of personal choice, yet the desire to communicate this particular message has been with us since the beginning of the conscious process to build. Architectural students are taught tectonics; the classical language of architectural elements and their visual expressions; the differences between members which are supporting and those which are being carried; and the differences between elements which act in tension and those which are acting under compression. It is easy to be influenced by technology, new methods of production and new materials.

Why are architects so keen to communicate through design their knowledge and understanding of structure, materials and performance? It could be simply the joy of new discovery, the realization of how things work – almost a childish cry of 'look what I have learned today.' At the same time it could be a more sophisticated attempt to introduce another system to architecture, an attempt to formulate rules and break down limits .

In an era in which communication and technology are attaining and extending their limits to an almost inconceivable degree, it is worth remembering that there was a time when only a privileged few knew how to read and write, and the great majority of people depended on their own interpretation of symbols embedded in stone, timber or mud for their education and enlightenment.
In spite of the achievements of civilization and the accompanying scientific and technological progress, we still try to communicate our scope and knowledge through design. It is fascinating for children and adults alike to look inside things to find out how they work. Knowledge of technology means progress, and through this knowledge people can (one hopes) improve their lives, achieve wonders and create values. More importantly, by controlling this process, they can widen their choices.

The notion of control over technology is seductive. Allow me to illustrate my point with an anecdote from my childhood. At the age of about three, my little friend was given as a Christmas present a beautifully painted timber bus and a big box of tools. While the other children were still occupied with unwrapping their boxes, my friend disappeared to his bedroom and quietly embedded all the new nails with his new hammer into the body of his new, shiny bus. He had altered the aesthetics of his new toy to achieve the effect that he liked and understood. The beautiful bus with all its hidden fixings and connections was – understandably, to his child's eyes – nothing more than a piece of timber, which he could transform into his own creation. Sometimes, I wonder if 'adult' designers are driven by a similar desire.

On a more serious note, I personally share with my grown-up friends a sometimes excessive admiration for technology, for the ever increasing knowledge of materials and their behaviour and properties, for the ability to control the design discipline, for the wonders of manufacturing. What a joy to design every single screw and nut, every little joint and detail of an element. The examples chosen to illustrate this fascination with technology show an extraordinary variety of ideas, tricks, skills and jokes. Even those who are more traditionally minded, or who dislike complexity for its own sake, cannot help but admire these projects if for nothing more than the inventiveness of their design and the perfection of their execution.

The glass-enclosed external escalator at the Centre Pompidou in Paris, by Piano and Rogers.

Jyrki Tasa /
Single Person's House /
Espoo, Finland /
1997

This little house was designed for a single person, but with space for entertaining. For this reason, precedence has been given to the ground floor living areas, which are connected to the two upper floors by a three-storey high plywood folded plate staircase. This is then suspended from the ceiling by very fine steel wires. The size of the stringer is incredibly fine and the attachments to the folded plywood are remarkably simple. Do not miss the detail where the transfer of forces between the hangers and the stringer takes place, or the way in which the horizontal elements of the balustrading meet their vertical counterparts. Stability is aided by the circular form of the staircase, but it does not surprise me when the architect claims that some visitors question the structural viability of the product prior to experiencing it themselves. According to the architect, the aim was to produce a modern design, using the beauty and softness of wood and the elegance and elasticity of steel. Clearly he has achieved this goal.

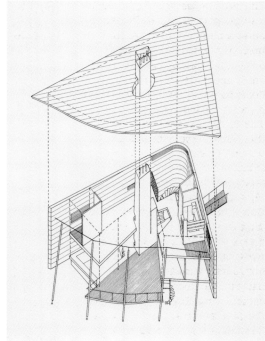

Opposite: When the staircase is seen from underneath its structure and system of supports can clearly be seen.

A view looking down the stairwell. From this angle the spiral appears almost unsupported, a source of worry to some visitors.

An axonometric diagram explains the spatial arrangement of the house. The staircase and curved stairwell is shown at the top right corner of the drawing.

The staircase is housed
inside a stairwell of
curved plywood, the
material also used for
the treads and risers.
This gives the stairs a
sense of continuity with
the rest of the house.

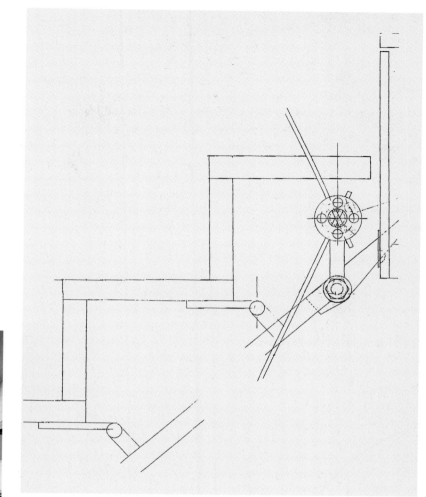

The stairs are supported, and kept from twisting, by a system of ceiling-suspended steel cables attached to the floor, stringer and balustrading.

Top: An elevation detail shows the system of attachments between the stringer, treads and supporting cables.

Above: Because the cables and attachments are so fine, they do not intrude on the overall design of the staircase.

Santiago Calatrava /
Volantin Footbridge Ramp and Stairs /
Bilbao, Spain /
1990–97

Santiago Calatrava is both an architect and an engineer and brings both of these disciplines to the design of his projects, which all bear the recognizable stamp of his combined genius. He plays with concrete and steel, and any other structural material available, with clarity and apparent ease. Calatrava's characteristic awareness that his structures are designed for humans, often a feature of his painted designs, is evident in this footbridge. The ramp and staircase leading to the footbridge are not just added afterthoughts – the ramp's triangular supports are what hold up the bridge's amazing parabolic arch. At night the ramp is illuminated from underneath the handrail to create an unbroken path of light from the ground to the bridge and across the river. A technical feat to be sure, but Calatrava never allows the details – the nuts and bolts – of architecture or engineering to get in the way of the overall design. It is no wonder that the bridge has become a landmark, a symbol of Bilbao's regeneration.

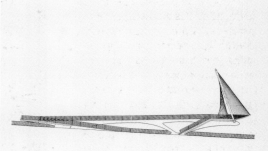

Opposite and above: The ramp and staircase not only provide access, but also form an integral part of the bridge's support structure.

The side elevation of the bridge illustrates how Calatrava has clearly expressed the distribution of forces in the ramp's design.

Santiago Calatrava / Tabourettli Theatre / Basel, Switzerland / 1986–7

Calatrava's staircase for this theatre and cabaret space may not be as large as most of his projects but he has created a large statement. Having spent so much time admiring the creations of nature and the bravura of 'shaping up' its structural components, I endlessly admire this zoomorphic skeletal structure. It is a man-made product achieving the highest possible level of perfection, beautifully expressing the structural performance with a flowing, organic, totally logical and expressive aesthetic. Calatrava's original sketch could be mistaken for a picture of a prehistoric animal; the realization is like that of a perfect sculpture, a monument to the total comprehension of technology and the ability to convey its secret meaning. The staircase acts not only as a means of reaching the upper level, but also forms an integral part of the theatre's structure by interlocking with a steel trestle, devised by Calatrava to support the ground and first floors of this medieval building. Even those who have no understanding of structural laws could not fail to pick up the inherent balance, harmony and perfection of this staircase.

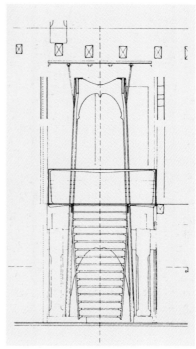

Opposite and above:
Views looking up and
down the staircase.
While the materials
used – glass and steel
– have high-tech
connotations, the forms
are decidedly organic.

The back elevation
showing the steel
trestle rising up
above the staircase.

The delicacy of the balustrading contrasts markedly with the sturdy steel trestle.

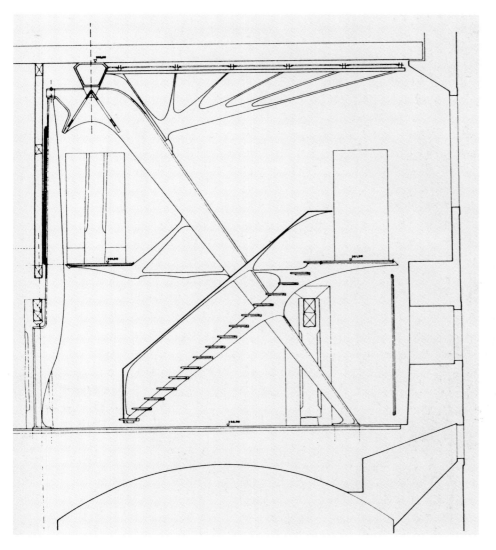

The wing-like supports shown at the top of the section transfer weight from the ceiling above onto the steel trestle, which then interlocks with the stringer.

Calatrava's original sketch typifies his organic style and demonstrates his extraordinary ability to communicate an idea.

Richard Rogers / Private House / London, UK / 1987

The main staircase in the house of High-tech guru Richard Rogers is a magnificent collaboration between the architect and the engineer Ove Arup & Partners. A perfect example of a staircase, it reads as a totally clear and understandable diagram of structural performance. The larger elements of the structure logically express the fact that they are under compression while the smaller ones understandably act as tension members. The handrail and its supporting posts are similarly differentiated from the balustrading cables due to their different functions. The treads of the stairs are manufactured in perforated metal, folded around the edges to increase stiffness. The connections and fixtures of the individual elements are as well designed as they are produced. On the material side there is certainly no waste, since, due to exact calculations, only the minimum amount of any material was used. As for aesthetics, the sheer simplicity and scale make the stairs appear very light, almost transparent, and practically weightless.

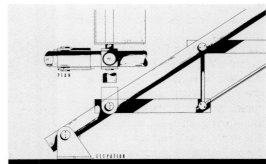

Opposite: The extraordinarily lightweight steel staircase leads from the airy living area to the mezzanine study level, creating a main focus for the space.

Above and right: The functions of the treads, stringer and attachments are as clearly expressed in the finished staircase as they are in the elevation detail.

John Young /
The Deckhouse /
London, UK /
1989

The metal staircase, which leads from the main living space to the sleeping platform above, is a freestanding object which, rather than being anchored to the floor, rests on wheels. This gives the staircase a sort of flexible character, and also increases its status within the space as a separate feature. Even an untrained eye could not fail to place this structure within the High-tech tradition. There is an obvious intention to express visibly the structural role of each element, and the application of these elements shows great skill and knowledge. There is, however, such an overdose of technical features as to be almost overwhelming. Sometimes – as I have realized many times – less is truly more. But if you are a novice in the staircase game, use this example as a textbook. It will tell you everything you always wanted to know about structural performance, structural connections, and understanding materials.

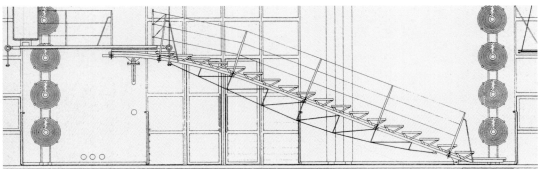

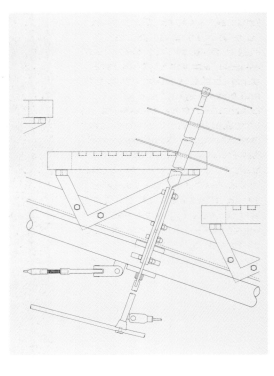

Opposite: The overall impression created by the staircase is one of complexity. The separate elements are differentiated by colour, size and material.

Top: The yellow staircase and contrasting red mezzanine level are presented as deliberately separate from the grey walls and floors of the space.

Above: Section of the main living area with the staircase leading to the suspended mezzanine level.

The elevation detail shows the connections between the stringer, balustrading post and treads.

Foster and Partners /
Reichstag /
Berlin, Germany /
1999

Some of us will remember pictures of the Berlin Reichstag in its pre-war form. Most will have seen the famous photograph of Russian soldiers fixing their flag to its top as a symbol of the end of the Second World War. From now on it will be the picture of Norman Foster's transparent dome that we remember dominating the German capital. Nobody will ever remember the endless discussions about the appropriateness of the proposal and the new interpretation of the massive dome of the original building. And in the same way that millions of visitors climb to the top of Saint Peter's cupola in Rome, so crowds will walk up the spectacular suspended twin helical ramps of the Reichstag dome. The ramp's 'floating' appearance is enhanced by its transparent curved glass balustrading framed by a simple handrail connected to the deck by a concealed clamp. The ramps lead to an elevated observation platform high above the assembly chamber. The high-tech aspects of the dome and ramp never override the obvious symbolism of the people climbing above the heads of their political leaders.

Opposite: The twin helical ramps appear to float within the new dome, an effect enhanced by the curved glass balustrading.

Constant movement created by visitors going up and down the ramps is one visual effect that cannot be controlled by the architect. This movement is multiplied by reflections in the the mirrored central column.

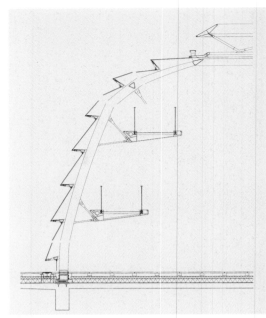

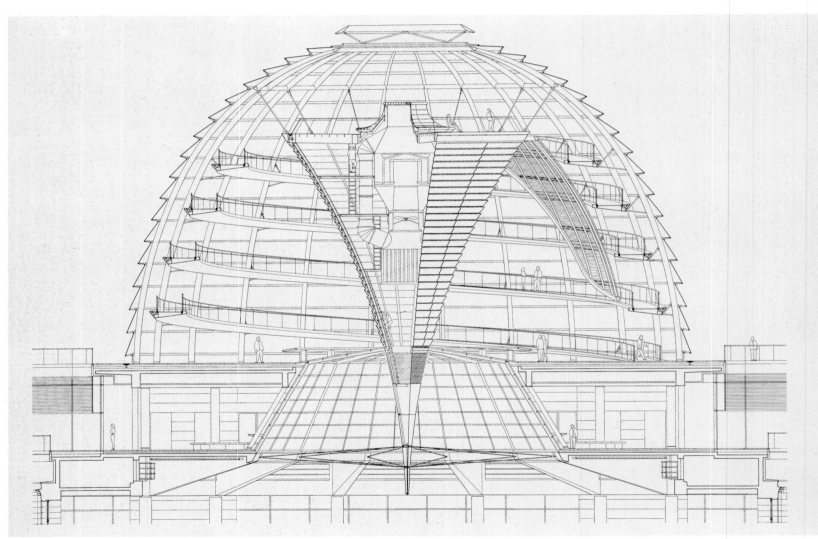

Above: A cross section of the dome shows the arrangement of the ramps around the cone-shaped central column.

Top: A cross section detail showing how the ramps are attached to the sides of the dome.

When seen from the
outside, the dome
becomes a complex
arrangement of
layers, reflections
and movement.

Nicholas Grimshaw /
Conway Street Office /
London, UK /
1992

Though the stairs in Nicholas Grimshaw's London office may use a different type of technology from John Young's (see pages 150–51), the design philosophy and structural principle are fairly similar. On the one hand, as in Young's example, there are no decorative elements – everything fulfils its function. On the other hand, the structure's technical complexity results in an aesthetic which is neither harmonious nor tranquil, and involves so much excess that the underlying logic is wrapped up in numerous layers of clever camouflage. Interestingly enough, Grimshaw's stairs have become as much his own trademark as Richard Rogers' have became his, mainly for Grimshaw's exaggerated use of metal castings.

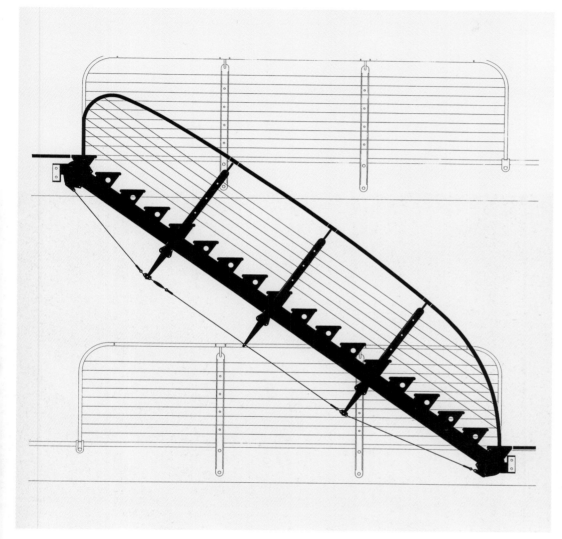

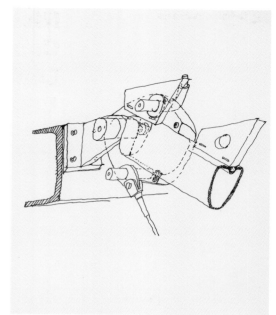

Opposite: The stairs in the Grimshaw office play an integral role not only as a means of circulation but as a central visual focus which can even be seen from the street outside.

The section clearly shows how the loop of the curved handrail is continued underneath the stairs by the tensioned cable of the stringer.

Top: A detail illustrates how the stringer is attached to the landing – a very complex junction designed down to the last nut and bolt.

Above: Looking up the stairwell to the underside of the flight above. While the stringer is very substantial, the rest of the elements appear comparatively lightweight.

Anshen & Allen architects / UCLA Faculty of Biochemistry / Los Angeles, USA / 1989

If the architects of this building did not associate its form with the institution it was meant to house – the school of Biochemistry – they certainly, consciously or otherwise, came up with a shape for the staircase and main stairwell that is considerably softer and more organic than the other examples in this chapter. The best view is from the top looking down the daylit stairwell, where the curves of the flights soften the effect of the hard concrete and provide an instantly understandable overview of the clever design concept. The details are subtle and the presence of a skylight creates a play of light and shadows across the concrete surfaces. The round skylight and the almond-shaped stairwell combine to create an unmistakable feeling that you are looking through an enormous eye. Generally speaking, American architects have not been as heavily infected with the High-tech virus as their European colleagues, which is why in this chapter they are represented by examples which differ so drastically from the others.

Opposite: Daylight penetrates the stairwell through a circular skylight at the top.

The form of the concrete staircase comprises, interestingly, straight flights and curved landings. The prefabricated concrete elements and their junctions are clearly exposed.

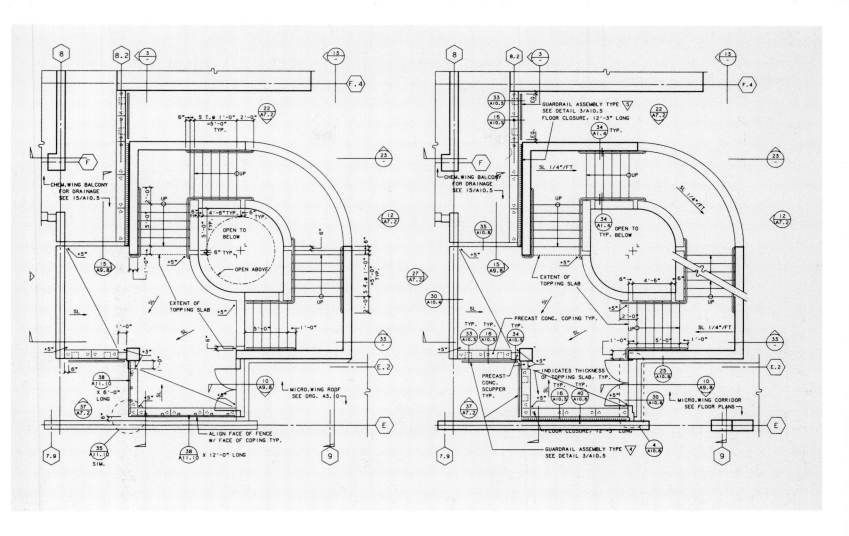

Opposite and above: The view up the stairwell and the plans show that the structure is based on an eye, with the skylight forming the pupil.

Rockhill Associates /
Library in a Private Residence /
Lawrence, Kansas, USA /
1997–8

The concepts behind this unusual residence in Kansas spring from the interests of the clients – mythology, philosophy, horticulture and science – while the appearance seems to reflect the agricultural buildings in the region. According to the architect, the clients' collection of scientific measuring instruments inspired the layout of the library, which is based on the shape and theme of the telescope. The library is a long, narrow space above the living area, and can be reached by a metal pull-down staircase, which itself resembles a kind of scientific measuring instrument. The library is seen as a place of quiet contemplation and study, and this separation from the living area is emphasized by the fact that the staircase can be pulled up like a drawbridge. Although it lacks the complex fittings and attachments of the Young or Grimshaw staircases, this example does share that conscious expression of technology.

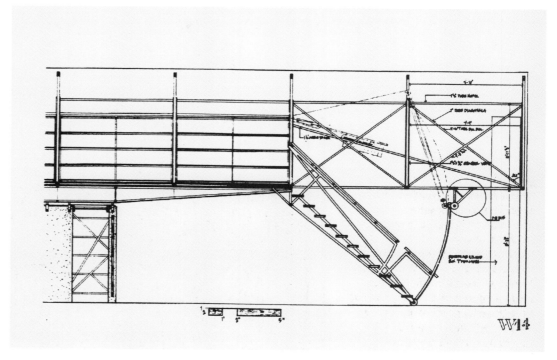

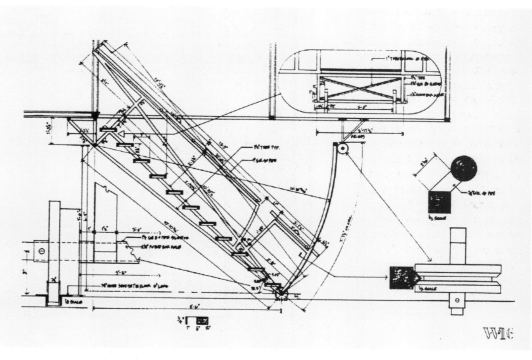

Opposite and above: The staircase appears to be an incredibly complex network of moving elements, metal bars and tubes, all of which allow it to be pulled up and down.

Top: The effect for those standing at the top of the stairs is rather like being at the end of a drawbridge.

Top and above: A section of the library and a detail of the pull-down staircase.

Richard Rogers and Renzo Piano /
Centre Pompidou /
Paris, France /
1971–7

Sydney would not be the same without its once troubled opera house and modern Paris would now be unimaginable without the Centre Pompidou. It feels strange that neither of these iconic buildings existed when I was younger – proof that modern architecture can become as symbolically powerful as an ancient monument in only a few years. There are hundreds of technical wonders contained in the construction and details. There is so much to admire, but the winning feature of this building must be the glazed outside escalators that move millions of visitors up and down, providing every one with the most memorable view of the city. Compared with the immaculate detailing of the main structure, you might be somewhat disappointed by the relatively crude undercarriage to which the cladding of the cheerful loops and curved see-through panels are attached. For once in my life I have to say it does not matter: the concept is so powerful that it overshadows everything else, details included.

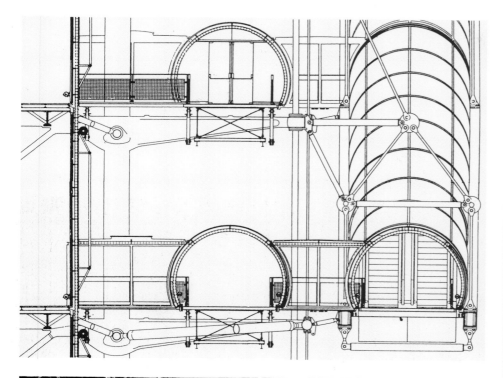

Opposite and above: The architects describe the building as inside-out, with traditionally internal workings presented as external features. The escalator tube is the most dramatic expression of this concept.

Top and right: A section through one of the galleries with the escalator tube to the right. The tube is suspended from the building's outer framework.

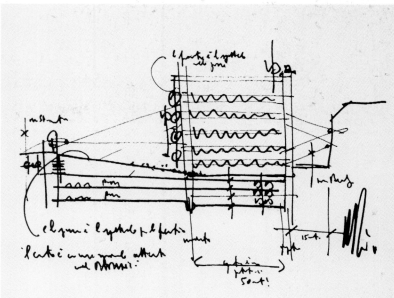

Opposite: Over 3,000
people an hour are
moved across the
façade of the building
through the 150-metre-
(490-foot-) long tunnel.

A sectional drawing:
the tube is represented
at each floor level by
a circle on the left of
the building.

less is more

less is more

There is a place for visual complexity in architecture just as there is a place for simplicity and clarity. Both have their roles, and both can be done either badly or beautifully. There is a common belief that the path to simplification is a rigorous one. The brain does not usually resolve a complex question with a simple, one-off answer; simplification is, generally speaking, the result of discipline, knowledge and control over the design process. It certainly does not come easily! In architecture, art and design there are unlimited choices. In the same way that designers can go for 'nuts and bolts' they can also go for 'next to nothing'. Minimalism is not exactly the equal of simplicity. It is an aesthetic philosophy which, in spite of its minimal appearance, requires maximum effort to achieve. The fact that the components of a structure are in tension or compression is not an issue. What is important is to create a result that functions – a device allowing the user to climb or to descend, but

visibly no more than that. No handrails? Regulations allowing. Fixing details? Certainly not. Structure? No one should know it's there. The aesthetics of 'minimalism' do not allow for the interference of expressed technicalities and related design references.

The compulsion to probe, to try to reach the very essence, the promised secret of hidden wisdom, is a natural element of our inquisitive minds. With minimalist staircases the concept itself is the main means of communication, and it is this that expresses the philosophy of purity and asceticism – the search for the essential. Because there is so little to be seen, every single detail, the quality of the material used, its textures and so on, play a more important role than with any other type of staircase. To those who are not spiritually minded, the message conveyed is that of simplicity, strict discipline, order, control, nothing superfluous. It is hard not to notice the veins in stone, the growth lines in timber, the imprint of

shuttering in concrete, the imperfections in cast metal. The stairs become an object of almost symbolic meaning, very often sculptural, artistic. The creators of minimalist staircases follow a path not unlike that of the heroes of High-tech architecture, trying to stick to the rules defined by one or another 'style' – and yet the results are so different. Function is not the only objective: aesthetic appearance is also an issue. The function of a structure can lead naturally to its form, but sometimes this natural result is totally overridden by the architect's design intuition and personal aesthetic principles. Another objective, for those who are not familiar with the building process, is that the level of production, skill, craftsmanship and all other factors involved in the process of execution are of the highest quality.

The staircase in the house of architect John Pawson epitomizes minimalism.

Peter Zumthor / Kunsthaus / Bregenz, Austria / 1997

Peter Zumthor's staircase in the Kunsthaus in Bregenz is more than just a means of getting up and down – it is a total spatial experience with steps. The stairs seem to lead to infinity, a concept expressed simply by the softly diffused light that penetrates the translucent glass panels of the ceiling. The staircase is situated behind one of the building's concrete slabs, and there are no windows. The architect has achieved an amazing feat of lighting technology by housing the entire building in a glass skin. This skin diffuses light throughout the museum via a series of mezzanine level light traps in the hallways, creating a daylit effect on all floors without any windows. The softness of this diffused daylight is complemented by the exposed, unpolished concrete wall slabs. The materials selected for this remarkably artistic statement – concrete, sandblasted glass and stainless steel – are strong and beautiful in their own right. If, when you reach the top, you look back down the stairwell you see a black hole, nothingness. What an experience!

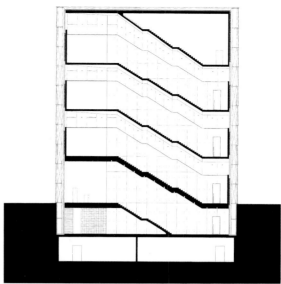

Opposite: The staircase sits between the building's inner casing and one of its supporting concrete slabs. There are no windows, but daylight is directed through the sandblasted glass panels that form the ceiling.

The unpolished concrete walls and grey terrazzo flooring combine with the diffused light from the ceiling to create a soft, almost blurred effect, broken only by the steel handrail.

Above and top: The building is enclosed in a self-supporting glass outer wrapper, which directs daylight into the interior gallery spaces and main stairwell.

Rick Mather /
Architect's House /
London, UK /
1978

Rick Mather's house in north London is one of the most unpretentious architects' dwellings I have ever come across. The top two floors of this typical Victorian row house have been ingeniously converted into a practical, attractive and very habitable live/work space, modestly referred to by the architect as a 'bedsit'. The living area is connected to the upper-level bedroom gallery – and ultimately the roof terrace – by a spiral staircase. The elegant, sculptural ribbon is painted white like the rest of the apartment, and in its simplicity it complements the architect's collection of early Modernist furniture. The stairs are neatly enclosed by the external and internal stringer, and covered in grey carpet. To simplify the construction process the the inside of the 'ribbon' is faceted rather than smooth. With my fussy disposition I would find it difficult to accept this less-than-smooth (but admittedly logical) approach. However, unlike many of his contemporaries, Mather does not seem to be interested in the expression of technology. Unpretentious statements are one of his strong points and perhaps the secret of his success.

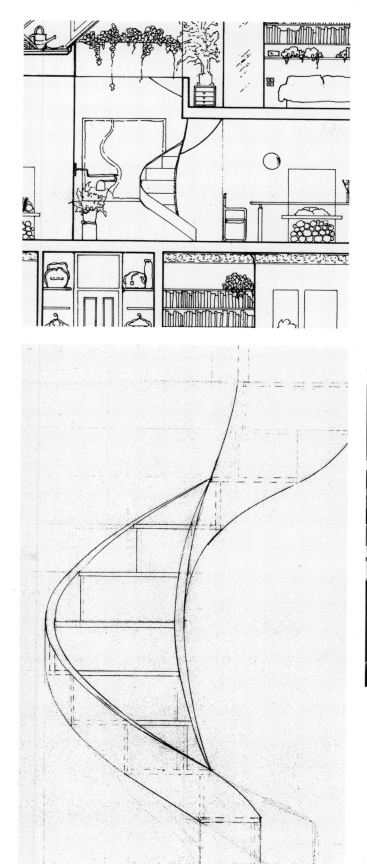

Opposite: The inside of the stringer is faceted rather than smooth, one solution to accommodating square treads in a spiral staircase.

Above and top: Drawings show that the stair was originally designed to be without a handrail, but one has since been added, presumably to meet safety requirements.

The staircase consists of a plywood stringer, treads and risers, which were screwed together and then encased in a layer of plaster.

Fumihiko Maki /
Kaze-no-Oka Crematorium /
Nakatsu, Japan /
1997

The staircase in this crematorium waiting area is a fine example of an object for which the visual expression has been chosen for a very specific purpose. The architect wanted to create a space that would allow mourners to be absorbed in their own private thoughts, an intention that did not allow for any excess, any decoration or egocentricity in the design. Fumihiko's modesty, evident in many examples of his work, clearly communicates a sense of humility and acceptance in the face of nature.

As the stairs lead down from a daylit mezzanine, the solid concrete balustrade turns into a horizontal platform. The balustrade, which acts as a structural beam, carries individual treads that appear to have no visible support or fixing detail. The handrail is little more than a black line, controlling the sense of direction and perhaps also lending a sense of support. The comforting presence of nature is alluded to in the use of timber for the steps, while the concrete of the balustrading is imprinted with the grain of the cedar boards used for shuttering. By contrast the rawness of the concrete itself expresses harshness and permanence. In this project nothing is superfluous, nothing needs to be added.

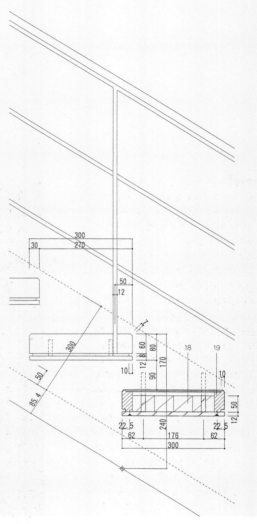

Opposite: The staircase leads from the waiting area to the mezzanine above. The combination of hard concrete and warm wood represents a transition between the solemnity of the ceremonial rooms and the natural world outside.

The heavy concrete supporting wall and thick timber treads convey a sense of weight and permanence appropriate to the building's use.

The timber treads appear to float on one side, but are in fact supported by metal frames which are inserted into the concrete handrail wall, as this section illustrates.

Jose Antonio Martínez Lapeña and Elias Torres Tur / Casa Mas / Barcelona, Spain / 2000

Until recently I had always associated the successful reconstruction of historic buildings with Italy. My own theory is that because Italians live cheek by jowl with such a plethora of historic monuments, they do not seem to suffer from the conviction that they have to reconstruct a building to its original state and possibly reinvent what might have been. They simply add where appropriate or do what their professional artistic natures desire. I have realized that this is also the case in Spain, particularly in Catalonia. The same principle seems to apply to Casa Mas. Martínez Lapeña and Torres Tur have created a little exterior staircase leading to the elevated front door of this medieval building in a way that could hardly be more modern or more minimal. Appearing delicate and sturdy at the same time, the staircase comprises a simply folded steel plate to form the steps, with an almost invisible mesh of balustrading. It is an interesting counterpoint to the very different but equally confident approach of Joan Rodon at Geltrú (see pages 116–19). What a courageous idea!

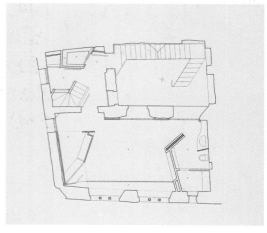

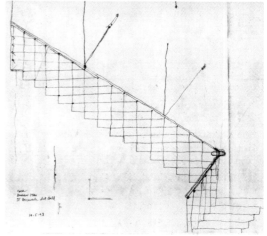

Opposite: The proportions of the elements – the thin steel plate and mesh balustrading – make the staircase appear fragile at first glance, but the unfinished texture of the materials lends it a certain toughness.

Above, centre and bottom right: The balustrading is supported by a single bracket attached to the wall (though two appear in the original sketch), while supports to the stairs are minimal.

Top: The staircase is shown at the top right of this first-floor plan.

Aldo Rossi /
Bonnefanten Museum /
Maastricht, The Netherlands /
1995

Minimal yet monumental, Aldo Rossi's 35-metre- (115-foot-) long staircase is the first thing that visitors see upon entering the Bonnefanten Museum. Perhaps the brick and timber that Rossi uses form a somewhat softer combination of materials than the other projects in this chapter, but the overall impression is just as strong. There are more design features then in the previous examples, which can draw one's attention away from the quality of the timber, the metal handrail or the high brick walls. Perhaps this particular case is not so much about styling as it is about the overall needs and philosophy of the place. The visible presence of light fittings, doors and pieces of furniture could be seen as a manifestation of humanity.

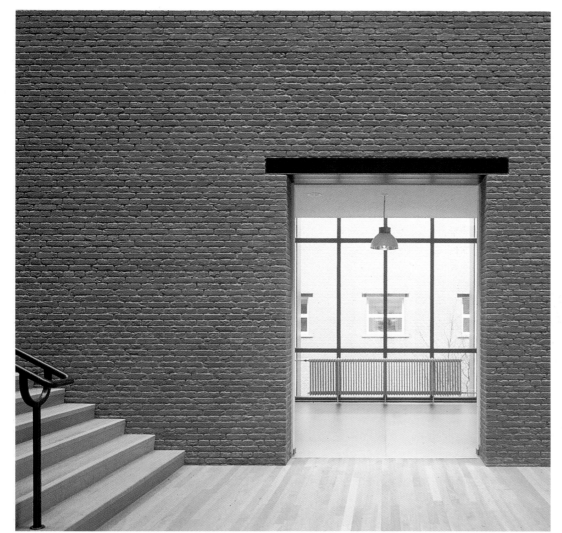

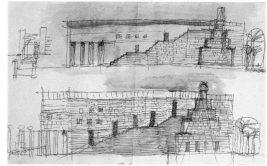

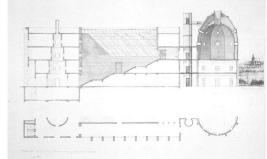

Opposite: The long, wide, well-lit staircase is the first thing visitors experience when they enter the museum.

The simplicity of the staircase's design is matched by the use of down-to-earth materials such as brick and wood.

The architect's concept sketch (top) and section (above) show the staircase as a progression of stepped planes that stretches the length of the building, not unlike the steps found at some ancient monuments.

Woolf Architects /
Private Residence /
London, UK /
1995

It took me a long time to decide whether the staircase in this residence by Woolf Architects should be included in this chapter. There is much more detail in the expression of the staircase's structure, and the design approach is much more visible. Finally I decided that the chapter would not be complete if at least one example did not show a staircase freely situated in space. There are two visible steel stringers with simple brackets carrying the aluminium treads. There is, however, no visible (or obviously hidden) effort to make a feature of junctions or connections. The simple elements form an elegantly unified statement. There is no monumentality in the usual sense of the word, except for the kind that can be found in anything aiming at a simple but strong design.

**Opposite and above:
Seen up close, the
aluminium and steel
staircase has a sturdy,
almost chunky
appearance, but viewed
in the context of the
main living space,
it looks delicate and
non-intrusive.**

Although the structural functions are clearly expressed, the connections between the stringers and handrails appear to be hidden.

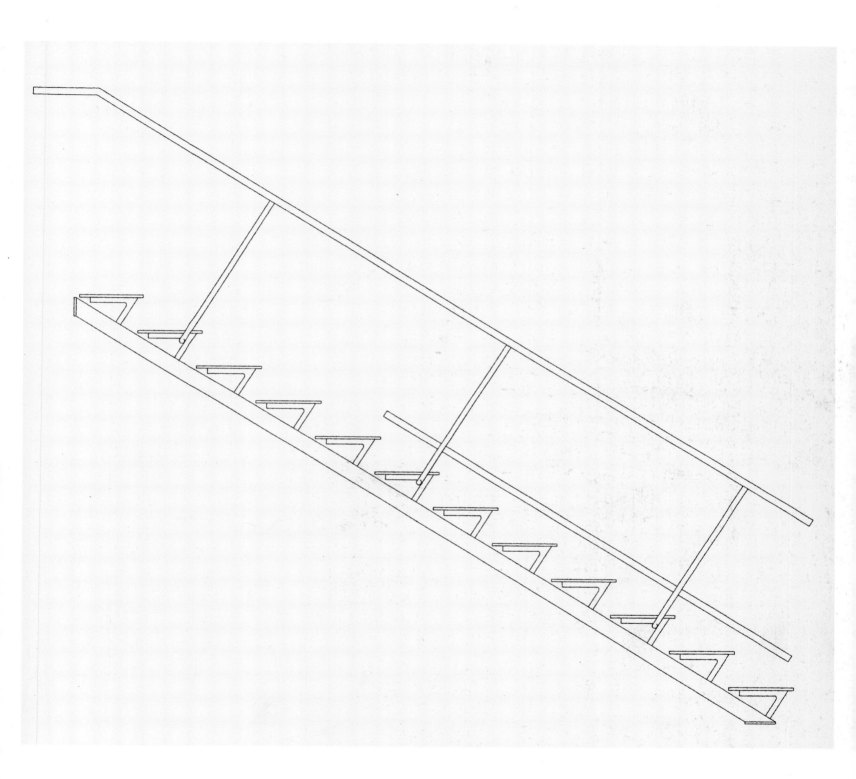

Above and opposite:
The architectural
drawings illustrate how
the steel stringers are
attached to the floor
and upper landing, but
not to the side wall,
enhancing the staircase's
floating appearance.

John Pawson /
Private Residence /
London, UK /
1999

Another example of a strong architectural space which almost incidentally encompasses a staircase is in John Pawson's own house. Visually, it is a stepped plane of limestone stairs spanning between two white walls. To create such an effect involves a complex structure. There is no handrail, and no obvious source of artificial light. A skylight and two windows at either end, with a slot in the wall indicating the landing, are only visible when you get to the top. There is no visible construction detail – an experienced eye must guess at what is hidden in the walls and treads. One could argue that it is a sculpture, so who cares what is inside! When descending you have no other option but to watch your step carefully, otherwise you may reach the bottom faster than you intended! Obviously a great effort has gone into achieving this stylistic perfection. Although in principle I have been a great supporter of the expression of function through design, I have to confess, along with many others, an admiration for the beauty of this masterpiece.

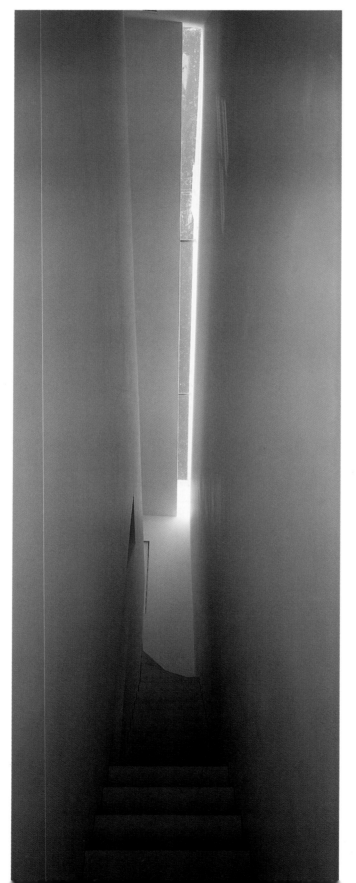

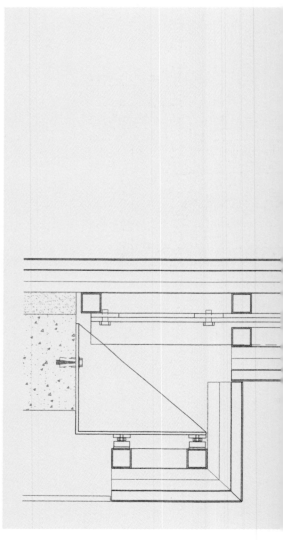

Opposite: As one climbs the staircase, the source of light – a thin strip of skylight – becomes visible.

Construction details are invisible from the outside – it is only through the section that the secrets of how the stairs are connected to the walls are revealed.

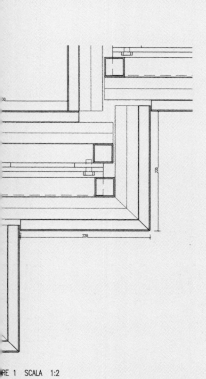

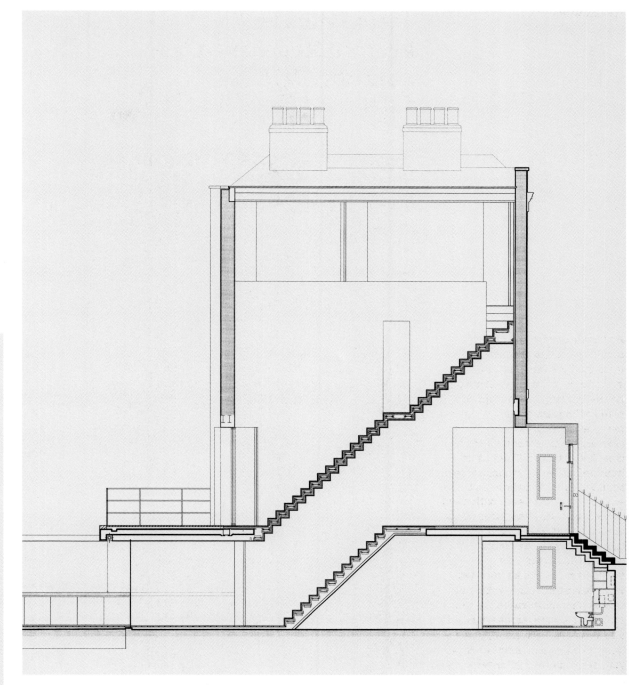

The staircase forms one
of the main features of
Pawson's conversion of
a typical London row
house. As this section
shows, the stepped
form of the treads
and risers is mirrored
on the underside.

index
picture credits
acknowledgements

index

picture credits

author's acknowledgements

With thanks to Gillian and all my colleagues for
having put right what I have done wrong as
much as for having put up with me generally,
to Tim Macfarlane and Matthew Wells for
collaboration, help and fun, and to all those
who have made it happen, as much as to
those who have paid the bill.